SpringerBriefs in Economics

More information about this series at http://www.springer.com/series/8876

Zoltan Acs • László Szerb • Erkko Autio

Global Entrepreneurship and Development Index 2016

GLOBAL ENTREPRENEURSHIP INDEX

GEN GLOBAL ENTREPRENEURSHIP NETWORK

Springer

Zoltan Acs
Center for Entrepreneurship
and Public Policy
George Mason University
Arlington, VA, USA

László Szerb
Faculty of Business and Economics
University of Pécs
Pécs, Hungary

Erkko Autio
Imperial College Business School, London
London, UK

Originally published by CreateSpace Independent Publishing Platform, Washington, DC, USA 2016

ISSN 2191-5504 ISSN 2191-5512 (electronic)
SpringerBriefs in Economics
ISBN 978-3-319-63843-0 ISBN 978-3-319-63844-7 (eBook)
DOI 10.1007/978-3-319-63844-7

Library of Congress Control Number: 2017947510

Printed on acid-free paper

This Springer imprint is published by Springer Nature
The registered company is Springer International Publishing AG
The registered company address is: Gewerbestrasse 11, 6330 Cham, Switzerland

Foreword: A Compass for Strengthening Entrepreneurship Ecosystems

The globalization of entrepreneurship has brought new interest and inquiries from thousands of actors new to the dynamics of the world's entrepreneurship ecosystem. As they attempt to leverage the power of new firm formation to create jobs and advance innovation, we have seen a massive roll out of new accelerators, educational programs, and policy experimentation – all powered by a sincere interest in creating the strongest possible local enabling environments.

With such increased investment comes a more somber responsibility to determine empirically what works and what does not in supporting a nation's entrepreneurs – or at bare minimum, to do no harm. Leaders in government, secondary schools and universities, nongovernmental organizations, and traditional businesses are eager champions, but they need more sophisticated research, robust data, and world-class analysis to help them efficiently direct their attention and funds to areas that will have the greatest impact.

This need has been behind the creation of the 160-country strong Global Entrepreneurship Network (GEN) and its platform of programs and initiatives that help any citizen to unleash his or her ideas and turn them into promising new ventures. GEN emerged from the community that created Global Entrepreneurship Week, an annual celebration that now occurs on nearly every nation on earth. While it started as a grassroots movement anchored in established economies with stable political systems, GEN has evolved and matured into a cohesive organization that operates in all types of economies and cultures. At the national level, GEN country affiliates lead local programs and initiatives ranging from efforts to inspire and educate nascent entrepreneurs to advancing research and connecting global leaders for face-to-face collaboration.

The Global Entrepreneurship Index (GEI) is of critical importance to GEN's ability to accurately assess and evaluate ecosystems in the countries where it operates because it collates comprehensive data on individuals' entrepreneurial attitudes, abilities, and aspirations and weighs these against measures of the prevailing social and economic infrastructure – thereby capturing the dynamic nature of entrepreneurial activity.

For GEN's country affiliates, the Index sheds light on the level of efficiency of national startup ecosystems through an analysis of 34 essential individual and institutional variables. It provides an overview of their entrepreneurship ecosystem and helps to reveal the bottlenecks that erode hard-won competitive advantages for startup ecosystems. By attempting to diagnose the key challenges that, if addressed comprehensively, would have substantial impact on new firm formation, it is an indispensable compass for developing strategic programs and new policy advocacy initiatives.

The need for comprehensive measures of entrepreneurial performance is also evident across governments and in the field of public policy monitoring and evaluation. To make the case for particular policy strategies and to monitor their peers, decision makers increasingly rely on numbers, charts, and rankings that compare national entrepreneurship ecosystems with one another.

New efforts in the field of entrepreneurship to quantify public policy performance and compare it with the goals of other governments must be guided by constantly improved research. While there are limitations such as imperfect data sources and the lack of standardized methodologies, GEI is able to translate and transform a wide scope of datasets into useful, actionable information for program and policy development. Thus, GEI provides leaders with an initial go-to analytical resource to begin the process of developing new policies that accelerate new firm formation, innovation, and job creation.

Of particular significance to policymakers, this year's edition of the Index offers evidence that entrepreneurship is a "global good" as it is highly correlated with bigger-picture human welfare goals such as increased economic growth, reduced income inequality, enhanced environmental quality, and wider political stability and security. Because entrepreneurship does not merely transfer existing wealth from one group to another but rather it "grows the pie" by increasing the total amount of economic activity that produces more jobs and more income for more people, the data provide evidence that entrepreneurs are a force for peace, equality, and expanded human welfare.

Naturally there remains an evolving list of global challenges – poverty, access to education, youth unemployment, and climate change to name a few – in dire need of ongoing cycles of innovation. The GEI shows that entrepreneurial activity in the world currently sits at 52%, meaning that we are only at about half of our entrepreneurial capacity.

Put simply, the world needs more entrepreneurs.

These are exciting times, as a new generation of risk takers is leveling the playing field and creating new opportunities for more people.

Jonathan Ortmans
President, Global Entrepreneurship Network

Acknowledgments

We would like to thank Ainsley Lloyd for producing the 2016 Global Entrepreneurship Index. She managed the entire production process from start to finish, including the country tables, the artwork, the layout, editing, and proofreading.

We would like to thank Jonathan Ortmans and Global Entrepreneurship Network for their support and collaboration on the production and dissemination of the 2016 Global Entrepreneurship Index (GEI) – encouraging policy discussions on these findings in every country included in the GEI.

About the Global Entrepreneurship and Development Institute

The Global Entrepreneurship and Development Institute (GEDI Institute) is a research organization that advances knowledge on links between entrepreneurship, economic development, and prosperity. The Institute was founded by leading entrepreneurship scholars from George Mason University, University of Pécs, and Imperial College London. The flagship project of the Institute is the Global Entrepreneurship Index (GEI), a breakthrough advance in measuring the quality and dynamics of entrepreneurship ecosystems at a national and regional level. The GEI methodology, on which the data in this report is based, has been validated by rigorous academic peer review and has been widely reported in the media, including in *The Economist, The Wall Street Journal, Financial Times,* and *Forbes.*

Zoltan Acs
Founder and President, the GEDI Institute

Global Entrepreneurship in 2016

Global Entrepreneurship in 2016

GLOBAL ENTREPRENEURSHIP INDEX

Top performers by region

#1 The **United States** (#1) is at a historical high of 86.2

#4 **Denmark** (#4) leads **Europe** at 76.0

#16 **Chile** (#16) tops the **South and Central America and Caribbean** region at 62.1

#19 The **United Arab Emirates** (#19) tops the **Middle East/North Africa** region at 61.8

#52 **South Africa** (#52) leads **Sub-Saharan Africa** at 38.5

Rank	Country	GEI
1	United States	86.2
2	Canada	79.5
3	Australia	78.0
4	Denmark	76.0
5	Sweden	75.9
6	Taiwan	69.7
7	Iceland	68.9
8	Switzerland	67.8
9	United Kingdom	67.7
10	France	66.4

Asia-Pacific
Increase export-focus among entrepreneurs

Europe
Help individuals perceive entrepreneurship opportunities

Middle East / North Africa
Reduce overall business risk

North America
Improve the visibility of entrepreneurs in their communities

South and Central America / Caribbean
Invest to develop new technology from within the region

Sub-Saharan Africa
Support post-secondary education

52%

The world is at 52% of its entrepreneurial capacity

Biggest one year gains

Indonesia 8%

6% Denmark, Sweden, Hungary

www.thegedi.org

Contents

List of Figures

List of Tables

Chapter 1
Introduction to the Global Entrepreneurship Index

The Global Entrepreneurship Index provides a detailed look at the health of nations' entrepreneurial ecosystems. We have developed an index methodology that links countries' entrepreneurial framework conditions with individual-level entrepreneurial attitudes, abilities, and aspirations. Our composite index gives policymakers a tool for understanding the entrepreneurial strengths and weaknesses of their countries, thereby enabling them to implement policies that foster productive entrepreneurship. The GEI is designed to help governments harness the power of entrepreneurship for sustainable economic development.

The GEI measures the quality and the scale of the entrepreneurial process in 132 countries around the world. It provides a rich understanding of entrepreneurship in these countries and a precise view of the strengths and bottlenecks of their respective entrepreneurial ecosystems. The GEI data are supported by three decades of research into entrepreneurship.

The GEI is a joint project with the Global Entrepreneurship Network, a platform of programs and initiatives aimed at creating one global entrepreneurial ecosystem. Ranging from efforts to inspire and educate nascent entrepreneurs to advancing research and connecting global leaders in person, GEN helps people in 160 countries unleash their ideas and turn them into promising new ventures that create jobs, accelerate innovation and strengthen economic stability around the world.

Since the number of countries in the GEI has grown, we are now able to provide regional information. This includes entrepreneurial progress in Africa, where entrepreneurship is rapidly gaining momentum and where the needs differ from those of regions such as Western Europe.

Distinct from both output-based entrepreneurship indexes (i.e., new firm counts) and framework-based indexes (i.e., comparisons of countries' policies and regulations), the GEI is designed to profile national entrepreneurial ecosystems. The GEI is not a simple count of, say, new firm registrations, nor is it an exercise in policy benchmarking. The GEI does not focus exclusively on high-growth entrepreneurship; it also considers the characteristics of entrepreneurship that enhance productivity: innovation, market expansion, being growth oriented, and having an

Z. Acs et al., *Global Entrepreneurship and Development Index 2016*,
SpringerBriefs in Economics, DOI 10.1007/978-3-319-63844-7_1

international outlook. Because entrepreneurship can have both economic and social consequences for the individual, the GEI captures the dynamic, institutionally embedded interactions between the individual-level attitudes, abilities, and aspirations that drive productive entrepreneurship.

Finally, the GEI recognizes that entrepreneurship can mean very different things in different economic and institutional contexts. A local horticultural venture, for example, would have different economic consequences for the Kenyan economy than a social media startup for Silicon Valley. Recognizing these differences, the GEI combines individual-level data with data that describe national institutions, as well as economic and demographic structures, to provide an institutionally-embedded view of the drivers of productive entrepreneurship (Fig. 1.1).

Fig. 1.1 GEI model of entrepreneurial ecosystems

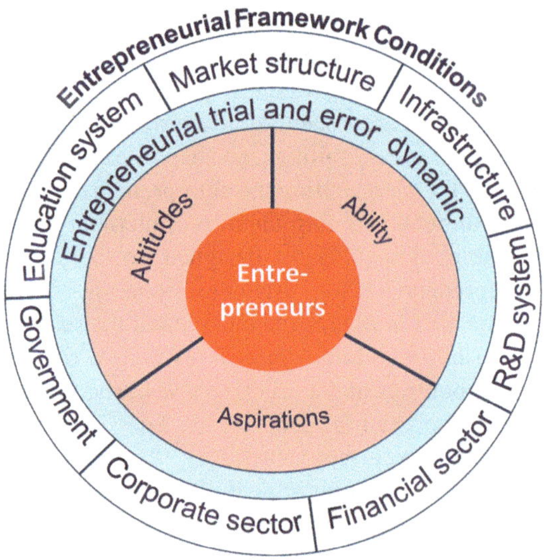

Chapter 2
Entrepreneurship and the Future of Economic Prosperity

2.1 Shaping the World of 2050

Last year we pointed out an important challenge for the future of the global economy: Whereas rich countries will be challenged to increase their economic productivity to sustain current standards of living as their populations rapidly age, low-income economies will need to integrate more than two billion young adults into the world economy by 2050. Economic initiatives by enterprising individuals are likely to be key in addressing the challenges of long-term productivity in rich countries, whereas poor countries will continue to struggle to integrate their rapidly growing populations into their economies.

How can more than one billion jobs be created in the developing world within this timeframe, especially in the least developed countries, where poverty and massive unemployment are already the dominant facts of economic life? The one solution that can provide jobs on that scale lies in a combination of innovation and entrepreneurship. Research on economic growth over the last 30 years has strongly emphasized that rapid job creation comes from rapidly growing companies. Therefore, the world's developing countries will be able to provide the jobs their rapidly increasing populations require only by encouraging the founding of companies that grow rapidly by providing widely desired new products or services. Such companies are usually created by exploiting new market niches and offering novel products, services, or processes that have few competitors or substitutes. The combination of novel products, few immediate competitors, and high demand created by new markets can sustain high levels of profitability, which will provide the capital and the incentives for the rapid expansion of production and employment.

This line of thinking points toward young entrepreneurs as the solution for both economic growth and job creation—and trends since 2007 have shown that this much-needed growth in entrepreneurship, particularly among younger populations, is indeed occurring. Furthermore, the timing of these increases suggests that entrepreneurship was not merely a temporary response to high unemployment during the

Z. Acs et al., *Global Entrepreneurship and Development Index 2016*, SpringerBriefs in Economics, DOI 10.1007/978-3-319-63844-7_2

Table 2.1 Total entrepreneurial activity across age groups

Year	Age 18-24	Age 25-34	Age 35-44	Age 45-54	Age 55-64
2007	7.08	11.44	10.12	8.21	4.69
2008	7.56	12.62	10.47	8.39	5.25
2009	6.95	12.25	10.22	8.11	5.44
2010	6.42	11.02	10.06	8.35	4.72
2011	8.29	13.10	12.65	10.20	7.00
2012	8.19	12.86	11.20	9.11	5.79
2013	8.66	13.13	12.15	9.31	6.08
2014	8.74	13.65	12.43	9.57	6.36
Percentage point change (2007-2014)	**1.66**	**2.22**	**2.32**	**1.36**	**1.67**
M (change per year)	**0.27**	**0.26**	**0.36**	**0.23**	**0.23**

Note: The table above shows the percentage of each age group involved in Total Entrepreneurial Activity. Darker greens indicate larger numbers. Only countries with at least 5 years of data, including 2007 and 2014, were used to produce these calculations. Those countries were: Argentina, Chile, China, Colombia, Croatia, Denmark, Finland, France, Greece, Hungary, Ireland, Italy, Japan, Netherlands, Norway, Peru, Romania, Russia, Slovenia, Spain, Sweden, United Kingdom, United States, and Uruguay

recession but a more permanent shift toward entrepreneurship as employment—the increases visible in 2010 and 2011 have lasted through the present.

The table below presents Total Entrepreneurial Activity (TEA) rates by age group—that is, the percentage of each age group involved in entrepreneurship. Entrepreneurship rates vary by age group, with the highest rates occurring in the 25–34 age range.

Entrepreneurship has increased across all age groups since 2007. The largest percentage gains have occurred in the 35–44 age group (up 2.32 percentage points), while the largest percentage of entrepreneurs is in the 25–34 age group (up 2.22 percentage points). This confirms what we already know anecdotally: entrepreneurs tend to be young (Table 2.1).

The increase in young entrepreneurs has brought important innovations—the sharing economy, Google, mobile apps, "big data," and a digital world that is growing in size and complexity at an exponential rate. Young digital entrepreneurs are the economic power source for the future; their work will drive economic growth and job creation for the next generation.

This millennium's response to entrepreneurship is fueled by the first truly digital generation, which grew up with digital technology. It is second nature to them.

2.2 The Global State of Entrepreneurship

Contrary to popular belief, the most entrepreneurial countries in the world are not those that have the most entrepreneurs. This notion is in fact misleading. In fact, the highest self-employment rates are in low-income countries such as Zambia and Nigeria. This is because low-income economies lack the human capital and infrastructure needed to create high-quality jobs. The result is that many people sell soft drinks and fruit on street corners, but there are few innovative, high-growth startups. Nor do these street vendors represent business ownership as defined in many European countries.

In entrepreneurship, quality matters more than quantity. To be entrepreneurial, a country needs to have the best entrepreneurs, not necessarily the most. What the "best and the brightest" do is important, and to support their efforts, a country needs a well-functioning entrepreneurial ecosystem.

Entrepreneurial ecosystems support innovative, productive, and rapidly growing entrepreneurial ventures. They consist of multiple interactive elements, all of which need to be in sync in order for innovative and high-growth firms to prosper. These firms also need skilled employees. They need access to technology. They need a well-functioning infrastructure. They need specialized advice and support. They need access to finance. They need business premises. They need a supportive regulatory framework.

Entrepreneurship comes in productive, unproductive, and destructive forms. While productive entrepreneurship makes both entrepreneurs and society better off, unproductive and destructive entrepreneurship make entrepreneurs better off but leave society in worse condition. The GEI strives to measure only productive entrepreneurship that both creates wealth-and is scalable.

The map below presents a snapshot of the global entrepreneurial ecosystem (Fig. 2.1).

The top ten countries for 2016 show a pattern similar to last year's—high-income, mostly European nations. Because the scores in the highest range are so close, small changes in score from 1 year to the next can produce a relatively large shift in ranks among the top ten. For this reason, we present confidence intervals for the top ten.

2.3 Top Ten Countries

The results show that the No. 1 rank could have gone to any of the top five nations: the US, Canada, Australia, Denmark, and Sweden. Similarly, all five nations ranked sixth through tenth could have been ranked sixth, but none of them could have been in the top five (Table 2.2 and Fig. 2.2).

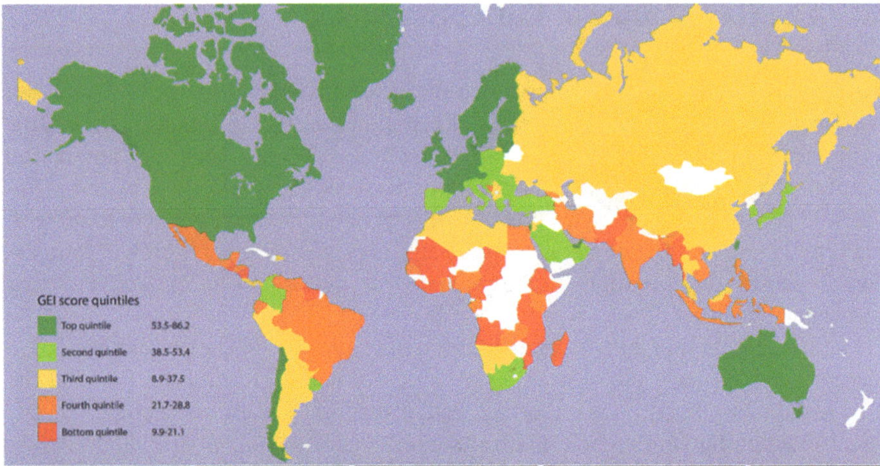

Rank	Country	GEI	Rank	Country	GEI	Rank	Country	GEI	Rank	Country	GEI	Rank	Country	GEI
1	United States	86.2	27	Korea	53.4	54	Montenegro	37.5	80	Iran	28.8	107	Guatemala	21.1
2	Canada	79.5	28	Turkey	52.7	55	Brunei Darussalam	37.3	81	Georgia	28.7	108	Guyana	19.8
3	Australia	78.0	29	Bahrain	52.4	56	Malaysia	37.0	82	Bosnia and Herzegovina	28.6	109	Pakistan	19.8
4	Denmark	76.0	30	Japan	50.6	57	Macedonia	36.6	83	Trinidad & Tobago	28.2	110	Nicaragua	19.4
5	Sweden	75.9	31	Slovenia	50.4	58	Costa Rica	36.2	84	Vietnam	28.2	111	Suriname	19.3
6	Taiwan	69.7	32	Spain	50.2	59	Kazakhstan	35.4	85	Nigeria	28.1	112	Angola	18.6
7	Iceland	68.9	33	Portugal	50.0	60	China	34.9	86	Gabon	27.8	113	Rwanda	18.3
8	Switzerland	67.8	34	Poland	49.3	61	Argentina	34.8	87	Mexico	27.6	114	Ethiopia	17.6
9	United Kingdom	67.7	35	Puerto Rico	48.1	62	Tunisia	34.4	88	Ecuador	27.4	115	Cameroon	17.6
10	France	66.4	36	Saudi Arabia	47.8	63	Ukraine	33.5	89	Egypt	27.3	116	Mozambique	17.6
11	Singapore	66.0	37	Slovakia	46.4	64	Jordan	33.5	90	Jamaica	27.3	117	Myanmar	17.5
12	Ireland	65.6	38	Oman	45.9	65	Thailand	33.4	91	Philippines	27.0	118	Gambia, The	17.4
13	Netherlands	65.4	39	Kuwait	45.6	66	Botswana	33.1	92	Brazil	26.1	119	Liberia	17.3
14	Germany	64.6	40	Hong Kong	45.4	67	Panama	32.4	93	Paraguay	26.0	120	Côte d'Ivoire	17.0
15	Austria	62.9	41	Hungary	45.1	68	Russia	32.2	94	Lao PDR	25.9	121	Tanzania	16.8
16	Chile	62.1	42	Romania	44.9	69	Bolivia	32.1	95	Swaziland	25.8	122	Mali	16.6
17	Belgium	62.1	43	Colombia	44.8	70	Peru	32.0	96	El Salvador	25.6	123	Uganda	15.8
18	Finland	61.8	44	Czech Republic	44.2	71	Dominican Republic	31.7	97	Sri Lanka	25.5	124	Benin	15.8
19	United Arab Emirates	61.4	45	Greece	42.1	72	Moldova	31.3	98	India	24.9	125	Bangladesh	15.2
20	Norway	61.1	46	Bulgaria	41.6	73	Namibia	31.3	99	Ghana	24.5	126	Burkina Faso	15.1
21	Israel	57.4	47	Uruguay	41.3	74	Serbia	30.9	100	Venezuela	24.1	127	Madagascar	14.6
22	Estonia	57.3	48	Italy	41.1	75	Algeria	30.5	101	Cambodia	23.0	128	Sierra Leone	14.3
23	Luxembourg	57.2	49	Cyprus	41.0	76	Albania	30.0	102	Zambia	22.8	129	Mauritania	13.2
24	Qatar	56.7	50	Lebanon	39.9	77	Belize	29.8	103	Indonesia	22.8	130	Malawi	12.4
25	Lithuania	54.8	51	Croatia	39.9	78	Morocco	29.5	104	Kenya	22.1	131	Burundi	11.9
26	Latvia	53.5	52	South Africa	38.5	79	Libya	28.9	105	Honduras	21.9	132	Chad	9.9
			53	Barbados	38.5				106	Senegal	21.7			

Fig. 2.1 Global Entrepreneurship Index Map

Table 2.2 Top ten countries in the GEI

Country	GEI 2016 lower limit	GEI 2016 upper limit	GEI 2016	Rank 2016	GEI 2015	Rank 2015
United States	91.4	81.1	86.2	1	85.0	1
Canada	85.5	73.4	79.5	2	81.5	2
Australia	87.4	68.6	78.0	3	77.6	3
Denmark	85.8	66.3	76.0	4	71.4	6
Sweden	84.6	67.1	75.9	5	71.8	5
Taiwan	77.0	62.4	69.7	6	69.1	8
Iceland	78.7	59.2	68.9	7	70.4	7
Switzerland	75.7	59.8	67.8	8	68.6	9
United Kingdom	71.8	63.5	67.7	9	72.7	4
France	76.8	56.0	66.4	10	67.3	12

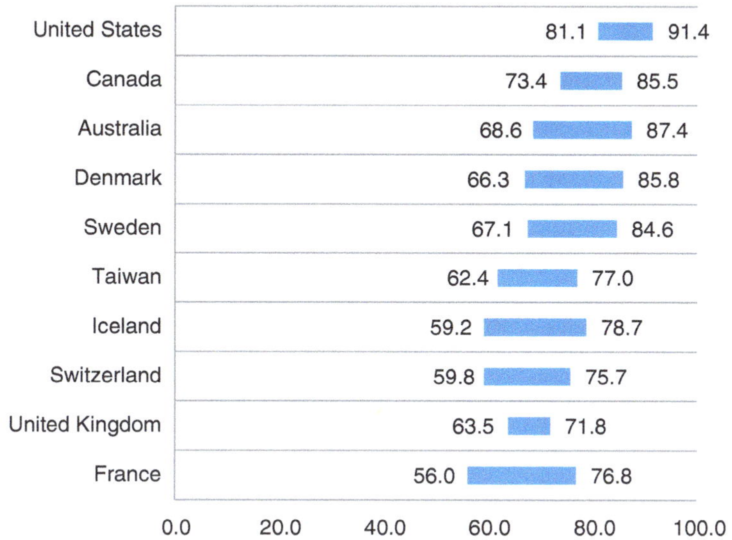

Fig. 2.2 Confidence intervals for top ten scores

2.4 Regional Performance

For many countries, a regional benchmark is more relevant for identifying best practices for fostering entrepreneurship. Below we present the top performer in each region, along with individual and institutional score summaries (Table 2.3).

The United States scores first in the world, and first in the North American region, just ahead of peer Canada. Australia ranks first in the Asia-Pacific region, ahead of economic powerhouses China, Singapore, Hong Kong, and Japan. Denmark, which ranked third in the European region and sixth overall last year, now comes in first in Europe. Chile ranks first in South and Central America and the Caribbean (16th overall), 19 places ahead of the next highest scorer in the region—Puerto Rico, at 35th. The United Arab Emirates ranks 19th overall and tops the MENA region, just ahead of Israel at 21st. In Sub-Saharan Africa, South Africa is the leader at 52nd, ranking ahead of nine European nations.

2.5 Biggest Gains (Table 2.4)

2.6 Biggest Declines

As entrepreneurship increases globally, what other implications could we expect to see? And what institutional factors are likely to be precursors to a dynamic entrepreneurial ecosystem? In the next section, we explore the relationship between entrepreneurship and other phenomena (Table 2.5).

Table 2.3 Top scores by region

World rank	Country	Region	GDP per capita PPP	Individual variables	Institutional variables	GEI
1	United States	North America	$ 51,340	76.4	92.6	86.2
3	Australia	Asia-Pacific	$ 42,831	70.8	86.9	78.0
4	Denmark	Europe	$ 41,991	71.4	89.6	76.0
16	Chile	South and Central America/Caribbean	$ 21,714	78.5	70.1	62.1
19	United Arab Emirates	Middle East/North Africa	$ 57,045	73.5	76.6	61.4
52	South Africa	Sub-Saharan Africa	$ 12,106	63.4	64.4	38.5

Table 2.4 Biggest gains in GEI score

Country	Score 2016	Score 2015	Difference in score	Difference in ranking
Denmark	76.0	71.4	4.58	−2
Sweden	75.9	71.8	4.08	0
Hungary	45.1	42.7	2.42	−4
Poland	49.3	47.4	1.97	−4
Indonesia	22.8	21.0	1.72	−17
Barbados	38.5	37.1	1.41	−6
Thailand	33.4	32.1	1.28	−3
United States	86.2	85.0	1.28	0
Peru	32.0	30.9	1.18	−4
Iran	28.8	27.7	1.13	−14

Legend: Includes only those countries that have participated in the GEM survey and do not have estimated individual data

Table 2.5 Biggest declines in GEI score

Country	Score 2016	Score 2015	Difference in score	Difference in ranking
United Kingdom	67.7	72.7	−5.01	5
Czech Republic	44.2	48.9	−4.65	9
Norway	61.1	65.6	−4.52	5
Angola	18.6	22.7	−4.11	1
El Salvador	25.6	29.6	−4.05	15
Finland	61.8	65.7	−3.92	4
Belgium	62.1	65.5	−3.43	1
Colombia	44.8	47.9	−3.19	7
Mexico	27.6	30.7	−3.03	12
Malaysia	37.0	40.0	−2.97	3

Legend: Includes only those countries that have participated in the GEM survey and do not have estimated individual data

2.7 The Role of Entrepreneurship in Global Prosperity

Another significant question on the minds of many is exactly how entrepreneurship correlates with the bigger picture. That is, do the things that most of the world is striving for—a better environment, economic growth, and world peace—coincide with individual initiative? If they do not, then this avenue of development may not lead to a better world by 2050. In this sixth issue of the Global Entrepreneurship Index, we try to answer that question in terms of the world economy and global society. To our surprise, we, find that entrepreneurship is indeed correlated with many other things that are good. While we have been arguing for a long time that entrepreneurship can change the world for the better, here we offer some evidence to that effect.

Entrepreneurship is widely understood as a means of "growing the pie"—that is, increasing economic activity to create more jobs and produce more income for more people, rather than merely transferring wealth from one group to another.

But how is entrepreneurship related to such aspects of human well-being as GDP, income equality, democracy, environmental quality, economic freedom, and peace and conflict?

In this chapter, we present entrepreneurship data compared to six measures spanning the economic, social, and environmental realms to show how these factors might work in tandem, or whether they exist independently of each other.

The table below summarizes the correlations between the GEI and each of our comparator variables: GDP per capita (PPP); income equality (GINI); digital evolution (The Digital Evolution Index, Tufts); environmental performance (Yale Environmental Performance Index); economic freedom (Heritage Foundation Index of Economic Freedom); and peace (Institute for Economics and Peace Global Peace Index) (Table 2.6).

We find that the most common economic measure, GDP, correlates relatively highly with the Global Entrepreneurship Index. However, with an R-squared of 0.58, there is clearly more to entrepreneurship than income levels alone. We also find that entrepreneurship correlates weakly positively with income equality, another common measure of concern.

As we move into narrower indicators of specific aspects of prosperity, we find the highest correlations between entrepreneurship and digital evolution and environmental performance (both 0.72). Less closely correlated are Economic freedom (0.51) and peace (0.34).

We find that entrepreneurship can broadly be considered a "global good," as it is correlated positively with all six of these measures. Entrepreneurship is therefore unlikely to undermine and rather likely to contribute to human welfare across many categories. Furthermore, many comparator variables show a relationship suggesting that these variables are necessary but not sufficient for a flourishing entrepreneurship ecosystem. There are other social and cultural factors that must exist if entrepreneurship is to thrive.

Table 2.6 GEI correlated variables with R-squared coefficients

GEI-correlated variable	R-squared
GDP per capita	0.58
Income equality	0.13
Digital evolution	0.72
Environmental performance	0.72
Economic freedom	0.51
Peace	0.34

2.7.1 Does Entrepreneurship Make a Country Rich?

The data show that high-income countries tend to have better entrepreneurship ecosystems, and vice versa. GEI scores explain 58 percent of the variation in GDP per capita. However, many other factors are also at play in the GDP game. Namely, countries with high mineral wealth (the Gulf States and Norway) have very high GDP compared to their entrepreneurship scores. Singapore and Hong Kong also have very high income levels compared to their (still high) entrepreneurship scores, a reflection of their high urbanization and concentrated economic activity (Fig. 2.3).

This suggests that entrepreneurship doesn't necessarily make a country rich but, rather, that there is more than one path to wealth. It is also true that high incomes are not enough to foster entrepreneurship; economic structure and cultural qualities are also important factors of a healthy entrepreneurship ecosystem.

2.7.2 Does a Pro-entrepreneurship Environment Produce Income Equality?

One criticism of the capitalist economy and its manifestation in the United States is the theory that, while capitalism produces high incomes for some, it also produces high levels of income inequality (Fig. 2.4).

Based on the relationship visible above, entrepreneurship, an important component of a capitalist economy, doesn't appear to produce income inequality. When the GEI is plotted against the GINI coefficient (a common measure of income inequality/equality), the relationship between the GEI and equality has an R-squared of 0.13—GEI explains 13% of the variation in GINI, and in a positive direction (more equality is correlated with higher GEI scores.)

While there are cases like the US, Israel, and Chile, where good conditions for entrepreneurship exist alongside relatively high levels of income inequality, this is not the global pattern. The Nordic countries are among the strongest performers on both income equality and entrepreneurship. These patterns show that an excellent entrepreneurship ecosystem does not necessarily produce high income inequality, but, in fact, good conditions for entrepreneurship tend to exist alongside better income equality.

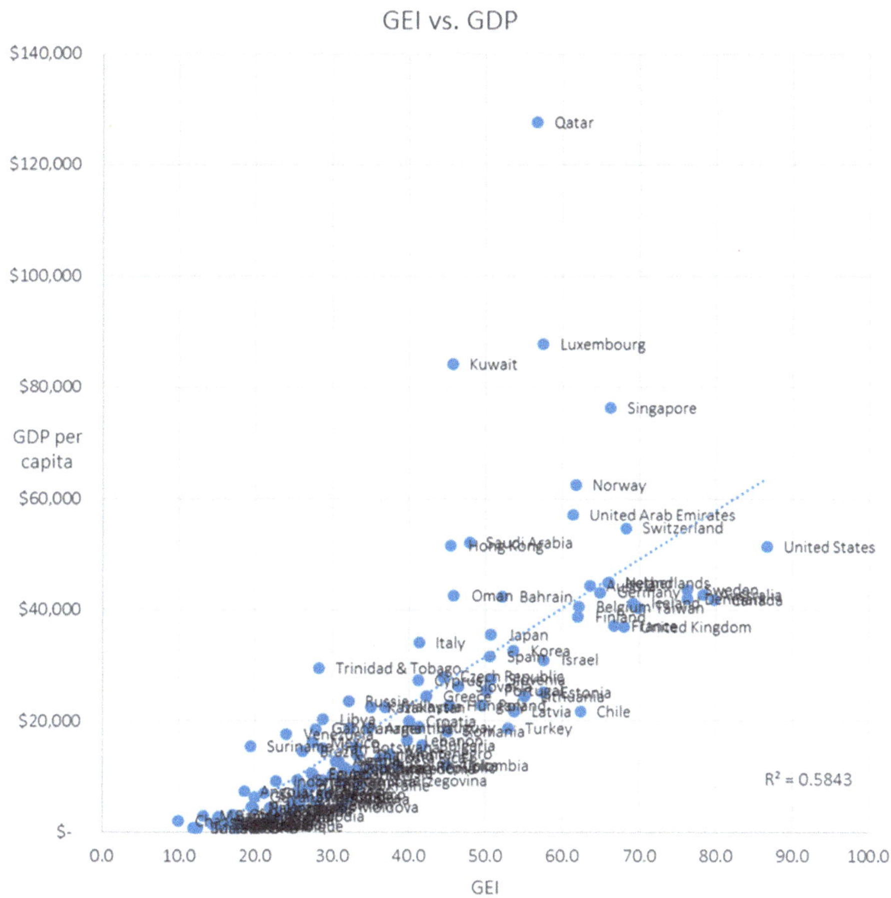

Fig. 2.3 GEI vs. GDP

The impact of colonial institutions also can be seen in this comparison. Countries in Latin America and Sub-Saharan Africa perform poorly in both income equality and entrepreneurship, which is linked to the colonial legacy of unequal wealth distribution between colonizers and colonized, and through economies that favored extracting resources over enterprise development.

2.7.3 Are Entrepreneurship and Technological Progress and Innovation Related?

Digital technology has the potential to transform the very way we lead our lives. It pervades everyday life at home, at work, at school, in our leisure time. Today more than one-third of all people around the globe are connected, which is transforming

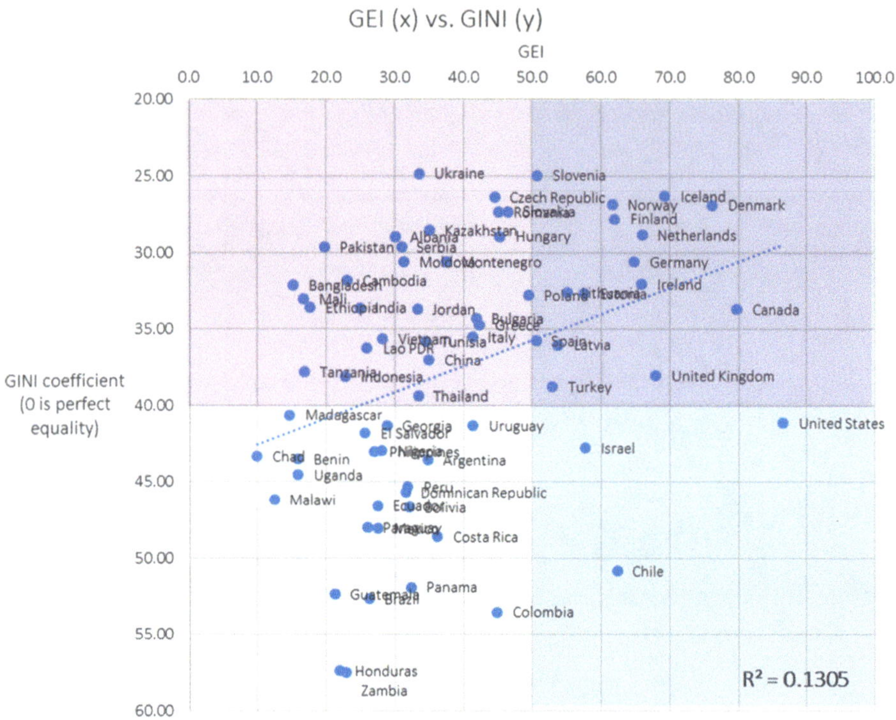

Fig. 2.4 GEI vs. GINI (NOTE: A GINI score of zero indicates perfect equality, so lower scores are better. For this reason the axis is plotted in reverse. GINI data are most recent value 2010 or later)

every aspect of the way people live—economic, political, social, and cultural. Digitalization changes how people live, how they share knowledge, and how they create, produce, distribute, and consume. It changes how citizens communicate with policymakers and how nations create wealth (Fig. 2.5).

The digital economy is powered by four industrial sectors: telecommunications, information technology, consumer electronics, and the media. Each of these sectors comprise various markets, and together they represent a large part of the world economy. Competition within and between these digital markets is fierce; companies from one digital market often enter and disrupt others. It is a fast-moving environment in which different firms move energetically into adjacent parts of the value chain in search of efficiency and market power.

At the same time, business models vary significantly: some services make money from advertising, often targeted based on data analytics; others are offered on a subscription basis. Many digital services grow rapidly due to low marginal costs and network effects. By contrast, digital infrastructure is characterised by huge investments and very long amortization times. This “entrepreneurial economy,” with its many different business models, is the biggest marketplace on earth, and it will be at the heart of tomorrow’s most successful economies.

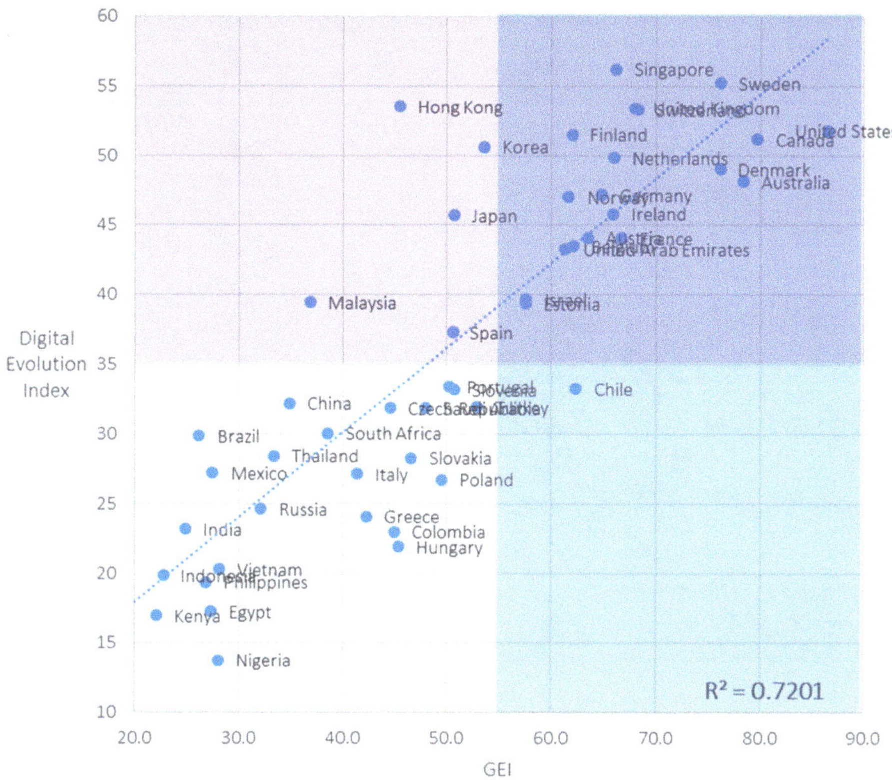

Fig. 2.5 GEI vs. Digital Evolution Index (The Digital Evolution Index (Tufts) "analyzes the key underlying drivers and barriers that govern a country's evolution into a digital economy: Demand, Supply, Institutional Environment, and Innovation." Data is from the 2014 DEI)

The data show that digital evolution and global entrepreneurship have a relatively strong relationship: an R-squared of 0.72. Countries that are highly digitally evolved tend to have well-developed entrepreneurship ecosystems. The East Asian countries of Singapore, Hong Kong, Korea, Japan, and Malaysia all have more evolved digital ecosystems than would be predicted from their GEI score alone.

Entrepreneurship and digital growth appear to be correlated. All countries that have high entrepreneurship scores have also developed robust digital economies: the United States, United Kingdom, Sweden, Singapore, Denmark, and Australia.

2.7.4 Does Entrepreneurship Destroy the Environment?

The positive relationship between environmental performance and entrepreneurship is the strongest of any of the relationships we examined—72% of the variation in environmental performance is explained by entrepreneurship. This is not to say that

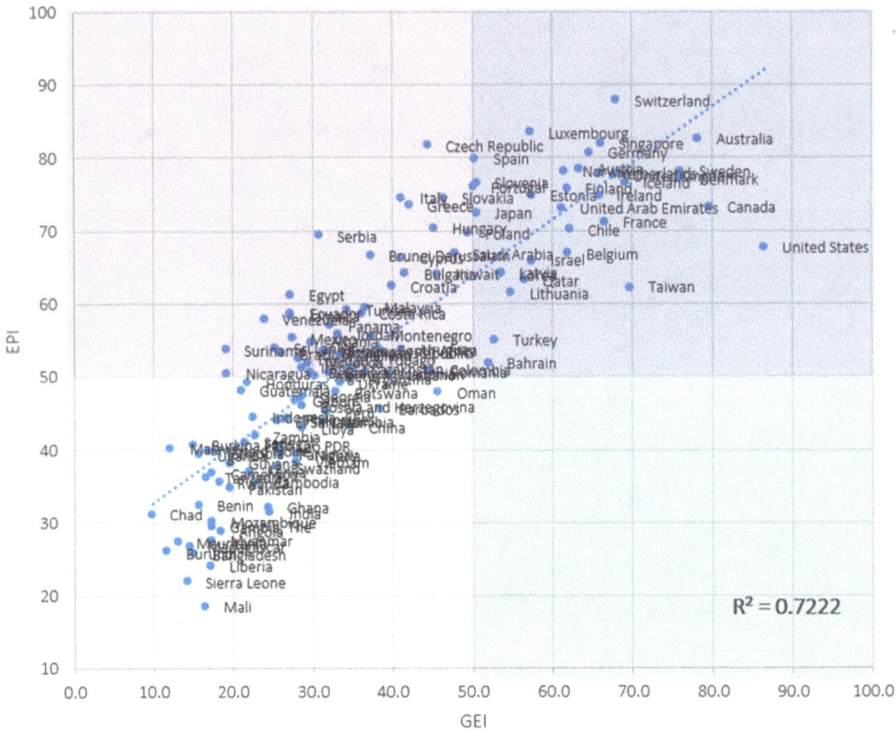

Fig. 2.6 GEI vs. Environmental Performance Index (The Environmental Performance Index (Yale Center for Environmental Law and Policy) "ranks how well countries perform on high-priority environmental issues in two broad policy areas: protection of human health from environmental harm and protection of ecosystems." Data is from the 2014 EPI)

entrepreneurship directly influences environmental performance, but that both are an outcome of good governance. Both indicators are driven strongly by policy, so the close relationship is not surprising—good governance is typically systemic, rather than limited to one government sector (Fig. 2.6).

We can infer from the shape of the data that the institutions that produce good environmental performance can—but do not necessarily—produce a good entrepreneurship environment, since there are no countries in the bottom right quadrant. No country scores well in entrepreneurship and poorly in environmental performance.

2.7.5 *Is Economic Freedom Enough to Foster Entrepreneurship?*

These results are unsurprising—despite a high level of economic freedom, East Asian countries like Hong Kong and Singapore struggle to translate economic freedom into a flourishing entrepreneurial ecosystem. Chile does very well at economic

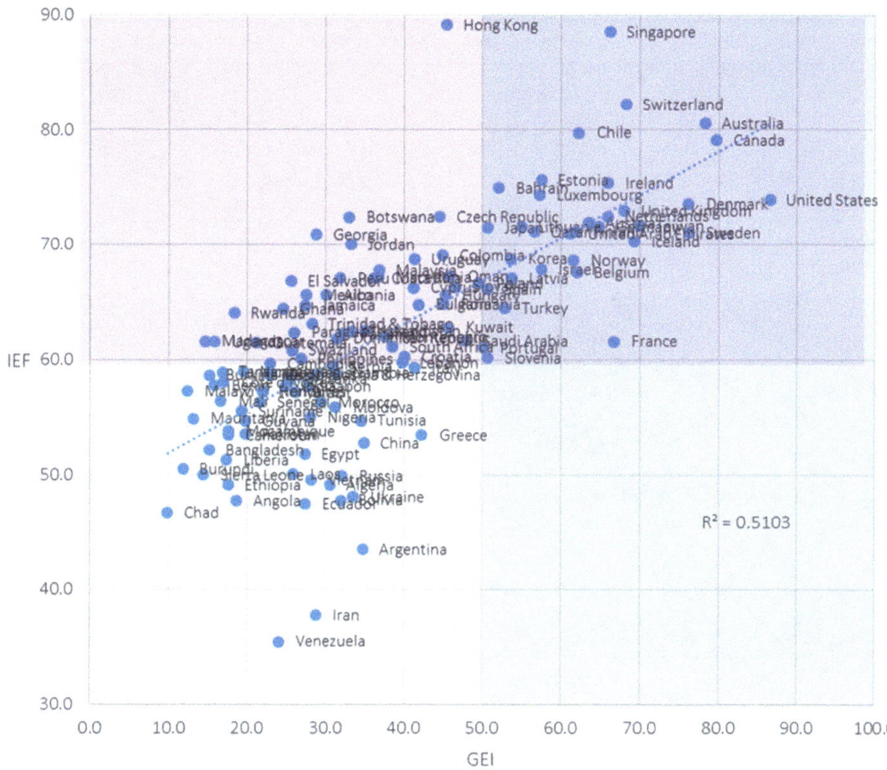

Fig. 2.7 GEI vs. Index of Economic Freedom (The Index of Economic Freedom (Heritage Foundation) measures economic freedom across four categories: Rule of Law, Limited Government, Regulatory Efficiency, and Open Markets. Data is from the 2015 Index. It should be noted that the GEI uses one variable from the IEF for Business Freedom. This variable has been removed from the IEF, and the IEF has been recalculated with just nine factors (rather than the original ten). The axis for economic freedom has been adjusted, since no country scores below 30 or above 90)

freedom, which explains some of its region-exceeding performance in both the GEI and the Female Entrepreneurship Index (FEI) (Fig. 2.7).

Economic freedom must be coupled with a culture that values entrepreneurship in order to incentivize individuals to become entrepreneurs. No country has a high entrepreneurship score and little economic freedom.

2.7.6 Does Peace Provide a Good Foundation for Entrepreneurship?

Much like the democracy relationship, we see that peace is a necessary but not sufficient condition for a flourishing entrepreneurship ecosystem: few countries fall in the lower-right quadrant, but many fall in the upper left (Fig. 2.8).

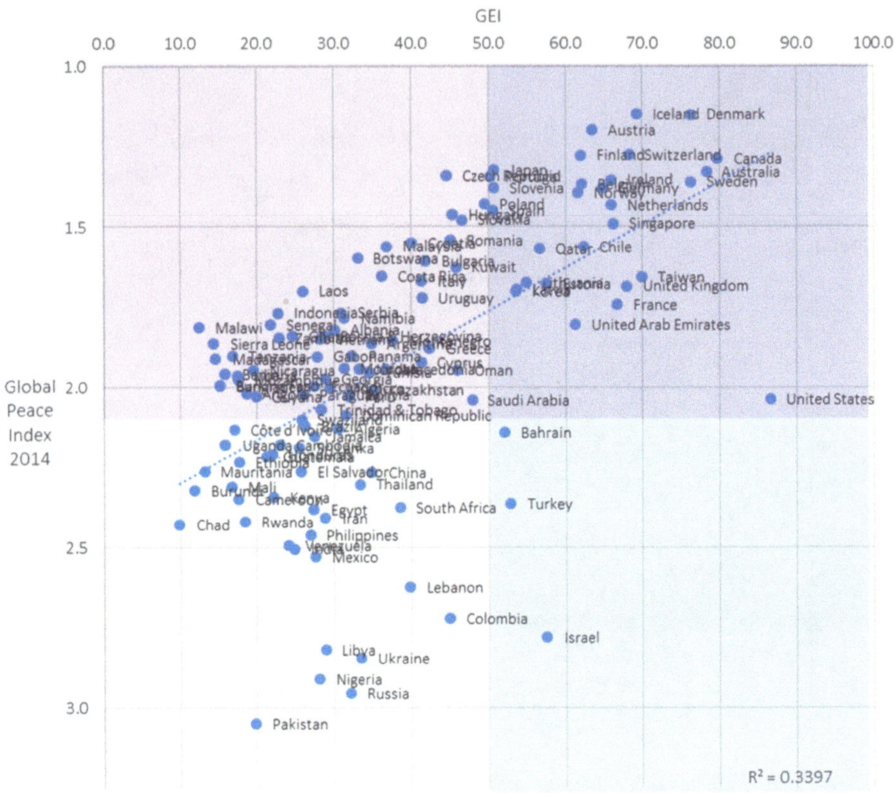

Fig. 2.8 GEI vs. Global Peace Index (The Global Peace Index (Institute for Economics and Peace) "gauges global peace using three broad themes: the level of safety and security in society, the extent of domestic and international conflict and the degree of militarisation." Note: The purple and blue boxes have been drawn at the midpoint of the range of data. Since the Global Peace Index ranges from 1.2 to 3.1 (for GEI countries), the midpoint is 2.15—it is not designed to put the U.S. in the upper-right quadrant, but nonetheless is having that effect. Data is from the 2014 Index)

One explanation for this is that stable, well-functioning institutions are necessary for entrepreneurship to flourish, as they reduce the overall risk for those undertaking the inherently risky activity of entrepreneurship.

2.8 Policies to Promote Global Entrepreneurship

The world is in a race for its very survival. If the population outruns our ability to create young productive entrepreneurs, the world will be lost. The good news is that we now know enough to create high-growth startups around the world. As one informed source puts it, we need to create about one high-impact firm for each 100,000 people per year in most countries in the world. Using the GEI as a compass and a roadmap can tell us both where to go and if we are on the right path.

Entrepreneurship ecosystems are complex. No index, however complete, can fully uncover the ecosystem dynamics. To achieve a full understanding, soft insights are needed from many different stakeholders, each of whom will be able to contribute their own perspectives to the debate.

The good news is that we now know how to grow entrepreneurial ecosystems and therefore how to create more and better entrepreneurs. We can do this within years, not decades, and we can track the results to devise even better policies. The GEDI's Regional Entrepreneurial and Development Index shows how a region can harness its own ecosystem and improve it. The GEDI's Telefonica Index of Digital Life helps us measure the intersection of the digital economy, millennials, and entrepreneurship.

Finally, the evidence we have indicates that productive entrepreneurial as measured by the GEI is associated with more good than bad. As US Secretary of State John Kerry said in Marrakech at the fifth Global Entrepreneurship Summit on November 20, 2014, and President Obama reiterated in Kenya at this year's Global Summit, entrepreneurship is the key to creating a better world for our children and their children. The world is now poised to take the necessary steps to create that better world.

President Obama noted that entrepreneurship has the potential to be a great equalizer:

- "One thing that entrepreneurs understand is that you don't have to look a certain way, or be of a certain faith, or have a certain last name in order to have a good idea."
- "The challenge is—as so many of you know—it's very often hard to take those first steps, like accessing capital or finding the right mentor."
- "It's even harder for women and young people and communities that have often been marginalized and denied access to opportunities."

Chapter 3
The Global Entrepreneurship Index

3.1 Introduction

The modern temple of the entrepreneurial ecosystem is like many temples of the ancient world: both are held up by pillars. Like the pillars of ancient temples—made of sand and limestone held together by cement—the pillars of the economic ecosystem are made of individuals and institutions that are held together by the "cement" of incentives created by institutions that influence the behavior of people. The entrepreneurial ecosystem rests on these pillars of development, which hold up three large building blocks consisting of attitudes toward entrepreneurship, entrepreneurial abilities, and entrepreneurial aspirations. The pillars must be of similar height and strength for a fully developed economy to flourish, and they need constant attention, continuous improvement, and careful maintenance.

In this chapter, we fully explain the Global Entrepreneurship Index. We start by discussing the S-shaped curve, followed by the 14 pillars of entrepreneurship. Country rankings and values are reported in terms of the GEI and these 14 pillars. We then present the three sub-indices of attitudes, abilities, and aspirations. Finally, we analyze and compare the different countries and country groups included in the GEI.

3.2 The S-Shaped Curve

Between 1945 and 1980, nearly 100 colonies in Africa, Asia, and the Caribbean gained their independence and began creating a development strategy for their citizens.[1] Sadly, many of those countries have experienced neither significant per capita

[1] For a review of the literature, see Acs and Virgil (2011).

Z. Acs et al., *Global Entrepreneurship and Development Index 2016*,
SpringerBriefs in Economics, DOI 10.1007/978-3-319-63844-7_3

GDP growth nor economic development.[2] Indeed, moderate to extreme poverty remains a significant concern for many developing countries.[3]

Hence, after failed attempts at development through import substitution and infant industry protection programs, and somewhat mixed results from export promotion strategies, developing countries are beginning to focus on their business environments and on creating economic spaces conducive to private enterprise, both domestic and foreign. Indeed, the promotion of entrepreneurship and the promulgation of small- and medium-sized enterprise policy have become important prescriptions for development in recent years.[4]

While a focus on entrepreneurship may seem a novel approach to development, it is consistent with and even complementary to older, more traditional development strategies. As these developing economies have moved from centralized economies to market economies, enterprise and entrepreneurship have become increasingly important. "The emerging world, long a source of cheap labor, now rivals the rich countries for business innovation. Developing countries are becoming hotbeds of business innovation in much the same way as Japan did from the 1950s onwards."[5]

In his classic text, *The Stages of Economic Growth,* W. W. Rostow suggested that countries go through five stages of economic growth: (1) the traditional society, (2) the preconditions for take-off, (3) the take-off, (4) the drive to maturity, and (5) the age of high mass consumption.[6] While these stages are a simplified way of looking at the development of modern economies, they do identify critical events. While focused on the age of high mass consumption, Michael Porter followed recent developments in the economics of innovation. Porter has provided a modern rendition of Rostow's approach by identifying three stages of development: (1) a factor-driven stage, (2) an efficiency-driven stage, and (3) an innovation-driven stage.[7]

Entrepreneurship is considered an important mechanism that promotes economic development through employment, innovation, and welfare, but it does not appear like manna from heaven as a country moves through the stages of development. Rather, it plays a role in all the stages of development and is a process that continues over many years. Economists have come to recognize the "input-competing" and "gap-filling" capacities of entrepreneurial activity in development.[8] In other words someone has to create the technology for new products and create the markets where people will buy them. Figure 3.1 shows the relationship between entrepreneurship and economic development.

The S-shaped curve addresses two important questions about entrepreneurship. First, the intersection of the S-curve with the vertical axis suggests that if individuals

---

[2] Easterly identifies the slowdowns in the economies of OECD trading partners of LDCs as a possible cause of the disappointing growth performance; see Easterly (2001), pp. 141–143.

[3] Sachs (2005), pp. 22–23.

[4] Ketkar and Acs (2013).

[5] Woolridge (2009).

[6] Rostow (1960).

[7] Porter, Sachs, and McArthur (2002).

[8] Leibenstein (1968).

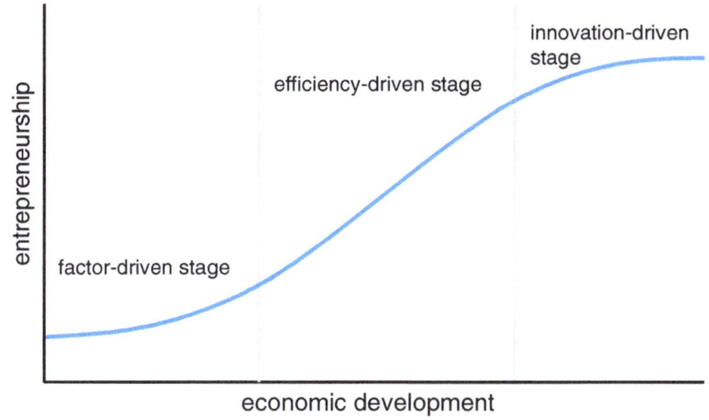

Fig. 3.1 The S-curve of entrepreneurship

in a country are very poor they may be in a poverty trap, where the chances for increasing income or wealth are limited. The S-shape of this curve represents the source of poverty. For those in the poverty trap, tomorrow's income will be less than today's, and any attempt to get out of this trap may result in even less future income, which helps to explain why the poor, and poor countries, are so little involved in entrepreneurship.[9]

The S-shaped curve also addresses the question of how much productive entrepreneurship there is in countries at different stages of development and how rapidly it grows. The other side of the S-curve, where it rises at a decreasing rate until it levels off, represents a situation where tomorrow's income is greater than today's, so entrepreneurial activity is possible.[10] How quickly countries modernize depends on the rise of this curve. The area above the curve is the "valley of backwardness," and being able to come out of the valley depends on improving a nation's institutions. As institutions become stronger, destructive and unproductive activities decline, and more entrepreneurial activity is shifted toward productive entrepreneurship, thus strengthening economic development.[11]

The valley of backwardness above the S-curve can only be eliminated by building better institutions and changing a society's incentive structure, all of which requires good government and governance. Our assumption of uncertain political economies means that destructive entrepreneurship is most likely to occur in developing countries with some degree of political instability, although it occurs in some form across most countries. As these unstable countries tend to rely on primary and secondary economic industries, inputs for activities in the tertiary and quaternary sectors are not of immediate relevance.

[9] Banerjee and Duflo (2012).

[10] Baumol (1990).

[11] Acemoglu and Johnson (2005) and Acs, Braunerhjelm, Audretsch, and Carlsson (2009).

The second source of backwardness is unproductive entrepreneurship, where we only take from one group and give to another. This form of rent seeking is prevalent in many developed and developing countries. If rent seeking by governments and other groups persists, entrepreneurs will be reluctant to make the long-term investment in time and money to create productive, high-impact firms. If countries have extractive economies where only a few benefit at the expense of others, development will not take place.

Therefore, we emphasize the effect productive entrepreneurship can have on the creation of social value as activity shifts out of destructive and unproductive entrepreneurship. In today's interconnected world, we need to improve institutions and be able to measure this progress.

3.3 The 14 Pillars of Entrepreneurship

The pillars of entrepreneurship are many and complex. While a widely accepted definition of entrepreneurship is lacking, there is general agreement that the concept has numerous dimensions.[12] We take this into account in creating our entrepreneurship index. Some businesses have a larger impact on markets, create more new jobs, and grow faster and become larger than others. We also take into account the fact that entrepreneurship plays a different role at different stages of development. Considering all of these possibilities and limitations, we define entrepreneurship as "the dynamic, institutionally embedded interaction between entrepreneurial attitudes, entrepreneurial abilities, and entrepreneurial aspirations by individuals, which drives the allocation of resources through the creation and operation of new ventures."

The GEI is composed of three building blocks or sub-indices—what we call the 3As: entrepreneurial attitudes, entrepreneurial abilities, and entrepreneurial aspirations. These three sub-indices stand on 14 pillars, each of which contains an individual and an institutional variable that corresponds to the micro- and the macro-level aspects of entrepreneurship. Unlike other indexes that incorporate only institutional *or* individual variables, the pillars of the GEI include both. These pillars are an attempt to capture the open-ended nature of entrepreneurship; analyzing them can provide an in-depth view of the strengths and weaknesses of those listed in the Index. We now describe the 14 pillars of entrepreneurship.

3.3.1 *Entrepreneurial Attitudes Pillars*

Pillar 1 *Opportunity Perception.* This pillar captures the potential "opportunity perception" of a population by considering the size of its country's domestic market and level of urbanization. A population's opportunity perception potential is an

[12] Gartner (1990), Davidsson (2004), Wennekers and Thurik (1999), all identify several dimensions of entrepreneurship.

essential ingredient of entrepreneurial startups. Within this pillar is the individual variable, Opportunity Recognition, which measures the percentage of the population that can identify good opportunities to start a business in the area where they live. However, the value of these opportunities also depends on the size of the market. The institutional variable Market Agglomeration consists of two smaller variables: the size of the domestic market (Domestic Market) and urbanization (Urbanization). The Urbanization variable is intended to capture which opportunities have better prospects in developed urban areas than they do in poorer rural areas. Market Agglomeration is determined by multiplying the size of the Domestic Market by the percentage of the population living in urban areas.[13]

Pillar 2 *Startup Skills*. Launching a successful venture requires the potential entrepreneur to have the necessary startup skills. Skill Perception measures the percentage of the population who believe they have adequate startup skills. Most people in developing countries think they have the skills needed to start a business, but their skills usually were acquired through workplace trial and error in relatively simple business activities. In developed countries, business formation, operation, management, etc., requires skills that are acquired through formal education and training. Hence education, especially postsecondary education, plays a vital role in teaching and developing entrepreneurial skills. Today there are 150 million students enrolled in some kind of education beyond high school, a 53 percent increase in less than a decade. People all over the world see education as a pathway out of poverty.[14]

Pillar 3 *Risk Acceptance*. Of the personal entrepreneurial traits, fear of failure is one of the most important obstacles to a startup. Aversion to high-risk enterprises can retard nascent entrepreneurship. Risk Perception is defined as the percentage of the population who do not believe that fear of failure would prevent them from starting a business. Business Risk reflects the availability and reliability of corporate financial information, legal protection of creditors, and institutional support of intercompany transactions.[15]

Pillar 4 *Networking*. Networking combines an entrepreneur's personal knowledge with their ability to use the Internet for business purposes. This combination serves as a proxy for networking, which is also an important ingredient of successful venture creation and entrepreneurship. Entrepreneurs who have better networks are more successful, can identify more viable opportunities, and can access more and better resources. We define the basic networking potential of a possible entrepreneur by the percentage of the population who personally know an entrepreneur who started a business within 2 years (Know Entrepreneurs). However, connecting through cyberspace with the rest of the world adds another dimension to networking and opens up much greater opportunities than before (Internet Usage).[16]

---

[13] Acs and Varga (2005).

[14] Papagiannidis and Li (2005).

[15] Caliendo, Fossen, and Kritikos (2009).

[16] Shane and Cable (2003).

Pillar 5 *Cultural Support.* This pillar is a combined measure of how a country's inhabitants view entrepreneurs in terms of status and career choice, and how the level of corruption in that country affects this view. Without strong cultural support, the best and brightest do not want to be responsible entrepreneurs, and they decide to enter a traditional profession. Career Status is the average percentage of the population age 18–64 who say that entrepreneurship is a good career choice and enjoys high status. The associated institutional variable measures the level of corruption. High levels of corruption can undermine the high status and steady career paths of legitimate entrepreneurs.[17]

3.3.2 Entrepreneurial Abilities Pillars

Pillar 6 *Opportunity Startup.* This is a measure of startups by people who are motivated by opportunity but face regulatory constraints. An entrepreneur's motivation for starting a business is an important signal of quality. Opportunity entrepreneurs are believed to be better prepared, to have superior skills, and to earn more than what we call necessity entrepreneurs. Opportunity Motivation is defined as the percentage of the Total Entrepreneurial Activity (TEA) businesses started to exploit a good opportunity, to increase income, or to fulfill personal aims, in contrast to those started by people who have no other options for work. The institutional variable applied here is Business Freedom, one sub-index of the Index of Economic Freedom. The Economic Freedom variable is appropriate for capturing the overall burden of regulation, as well as the government's regulatory efficiency in influencing startups and operating businesses.[18]

Pillar 7 *Technology Absorption.* In the modern knowledge economy, information and communication technologies (ICT) play a crucial role in economic development. Not all sectors provide the same chances for businesses to survive and or their potential for growth. The Technology Level variable is a measure of the businesses that are in technology sectors. The institutional variable Tech Absorption is a measure of a country's capacity for firm-level technology absorption, as reported by the World Economic Forum. The diffusion of new technology, and the capability to absorb it, is vital for innovative firms with high growth potential.[19]

Pillar 8 *Human Capital.* The prevalence of high-quality human capital is vitally important for ventures that are highly innovative and require an educated, experienced, and healthy workforce to continue to grow. An important feature of a venture with high growth potential is the entrepreneur's level of education. The Educational Level variable captures the quality of entrepreneurs; it is widely held that entrepreneurs with higher education degrees are more capable and willing to start and man-

[17] Guiso, Sapienza, and Zingales (2006).

[18] Bhola, Verheul, Thurik, and Grilo (2006).

[19] Coad and Rao (2008).

age high-growth businesses. The quality of employees also has an impact on business development, innovation, and growth potential. The institutional variable Staff Training is a country's level of investment in business training and employee development. It can be expected that heavy investment in employees pays off and that training increases employee quality.[20]

Pillar 9 *Competition.* Competition is a measure of a business's product or market uniqueness, combined with the market power of existing businesses and business groups. The variable Competitors is defined as the percentage of TEA businesses that have only a few competitors offering the same product or service. However, market entry can be prevented or made more difficult if powerful business groups are dominating the market. The extent of market dominance by a few business groups is measured by the variable Market Dominance, a variable reported by the World Economic Forum.[21]

3.3.3 Entrepreneurial Aspirations Pillars

Pillar 10 *Product Innovation.* New products play a crucial role in the economy of all countries. While countries were once the source of most new products, today developing countries are producing products that are dramatically cheaper than their Western equivalents. New Product is a measure of a country's potential to generate new products and to adopt or imitate existing products. In order to quantify the potential for new product innovation, an institutional variable related to technology and innovation transfer seems to be relevant. Technology Transfer is a complex measure of whether a business environment allows the application of innovations for developing new products.

Pillar 11 *Process Innovation.* Applying and/or creating new technology is another important feature of businesses with high growth potential. New Tech is defined as the percentage of businesses whose principal underlying technology is less than 5 years old. However, most entrepreneurial businesses do not just apply new technology, they create it. The problem is similar to the New Product variable: whereas many businesses in developing countries may apply the latest technology, they tend to buy or copy it. An appropriate institutional variable applied here is research and development (R&D). Gross Domestic Expenditure on Research and Development (GERD) is the R&D percentage of GDP as reported by OECD. While R&D alone does not guarantee successful growth, it is clear that, without systematic research activity, the development and the implementation of new technologies—and therefore future growth—will be inhibited.[22]

---

[20] Bates (1990).

[21] Baumol, Litan, and Schramm (2007).

[22] Stam and Wennberg (2009).

Pillar 12 *High Growth.* This is a combined measure of the percentage of high-growth businesses that intend to employ at least ten people and plan to grow more than 50 percent in 5 years (Gazelle variable) with business strategy sophistication (Business Strategy variable). It might be argued that a shortcoming of the Gazelle variable is that growth is not an actual but an expected rate. However, a measure of expected growth is in fact a more appropriate measure of aspiration than a measure of realized growth. Business Strategy refers to "the ability of companies to pursue distinctive strategies, which involves differentiated positioning and innovative means of production and service delivery." High Growth combines high growth potential with a sophisticated strategy.[23]

Pillar 13 *Internationalization.* Internationalization is believed to be a major determinant of growth. A widely applied proxy for internationalization is exporting. Exporting demands capabilities beyond those needed by businesses that produce only for domestic markets. However, the institutional dimension is also important; a country's openness to international entrepreneurs—that is, the potential for internationalization—can be estimated by its degree of globalization. The internationalization pillar is designed to capture the degree to which a country's entrepreneurs are internationalized, as measured by the exporting potential of businesses, controlling for the extent to which the country is economically globalized.[24]

Pillar 14 *Risk Capital.* The availability of risk finance, particularly equity rather than debt, is an essential precondition for fulfilling entrepreneurial aspirations that are beyond an individual entrepreneur's personal financial resources.[25] Here we combine two kinds of finance, the informal investment (Informal Investment) and the institutional depth of capital market (DCM). Informal Investment is defined as the percentage of informal investors in the population age 18–64, multiplied by the average size of individuals' investment in other people's new businesses. While the rate of informal investment is high in factor-driven economies, the amount of informal investment is considerably larger in efficiency- and innovation-driven countries; combining them balances these two effects. Our institutional variable here is DCM, one of the six sub-indices of the Venture Capital and Private Equity Index. This variable is a complex measure of the size and liquidity of the stock market, level of IPO, M&A, and debt and credit market activity, which encompass seven aspects of a country's debt and capital market.[26]

---

[23] Acs, Parsons, and Tracy (2008).

[24] De Clercq, Sapienza, and Crijns (2005).

[25] Gompers and Lerner (2004).

[26] Groh, Liechtenstein, and Lieser (2012).

3.4 The Global Entrepreneurship Index, 2016 Rankings

In this section, we report the rankings of the 132 countries on the Global Entrepreneurship Index and its three sub-indices. We also provide confidence intervals for the GEI s. The confidence intervals calculations are based on the Global Entrepreneurship Monitor (GEM) Total Early-Phased Entrepreneurial Activity (TEA) confidence intervals. Note that these confidence intervals only partially represent the potential measurement errors, as we do not know the full error term. In addition, we do not have information about the confidence intervals of the 34 countries where we use estimated data. In these cases, the upper and the lower limits are the same.

We present the rankings in terms of country development, as measured by per capita GDP. The overall ranking of the countries on the GEI is shown in Table 3.1. Like previous years, Anglo-Saxon, Nordic, and Western European countries in the innovation-driven stage of development are in the front ranks. The United States, Canada, and Australia lead the rankings. The big surprise this year is the fall of the United Kingdom to 9th place, primarily driven by declines in four individual level variables over a 3 year period: Educational level (among entrepreneurs), Competitors, New Product, and Export. While strong in attitudes and abilities, the United Kingdom continues to have an aspirational deficit, dropping to 26th in this crucial category. Three of the five Nordic countries, Denmark, Iceland, and Sweden, are in the top ten, and Finland is 18th—still a good performance. Taiwan, the highest Asian country, is in 6th place, and Singapore is 11th, which virtually ties it with France among the top ten countries. While the Netherlands maintains its 13th-place position, it is still among the world's most entrepreneurial nations. Besides their high entrepreneurial performance, these countries represent high income levels.

The United States is in 1st place. Australia, Canada, and the Netherlands are good performers, but they all have weaknesses in at least one of the sub-indices. Of the most populous EU countries, only the United Kingdom in 9th place and France in 10th place are among the top ten countries. The other large European countries rank in the middle: Germany is 14th, Poland is 34th, and Spain is 32st, followed by Italy in 48th place. While the UK, France, and Germany are relatively well balanced over the 15 pillars, Poland, Spain, and Italy are entrepreneurially less efficient.

A likely explanation for the EU countries' relatively weak economic performance over the last decade is their low level of entrepreneurship; the same applies to Japan, which took 30th place. Europe is still struggling to create new billion dollar companies. Factor-driven countries with low GDPs, such as Pakistan, Bangladesh, Uganda, and other poor African countries, are at the bottom of the entrepreneurship ranking, as expected. At the same time, these countries' entrepreneurial performance is the least unbalanced. However, some countries—including two former socialist countries, Serbia and Russia, innovation-driven Italy, and two South American countries, Brazil and Trinidad and Tobago—should have higher levels of entrepreneurship, as implied by their development trend lines, and more efficient use of entrepreneurial resources.

Table 3.1 The Global Entrepreneurship Index rank of all countries with confidence intervals, 2016

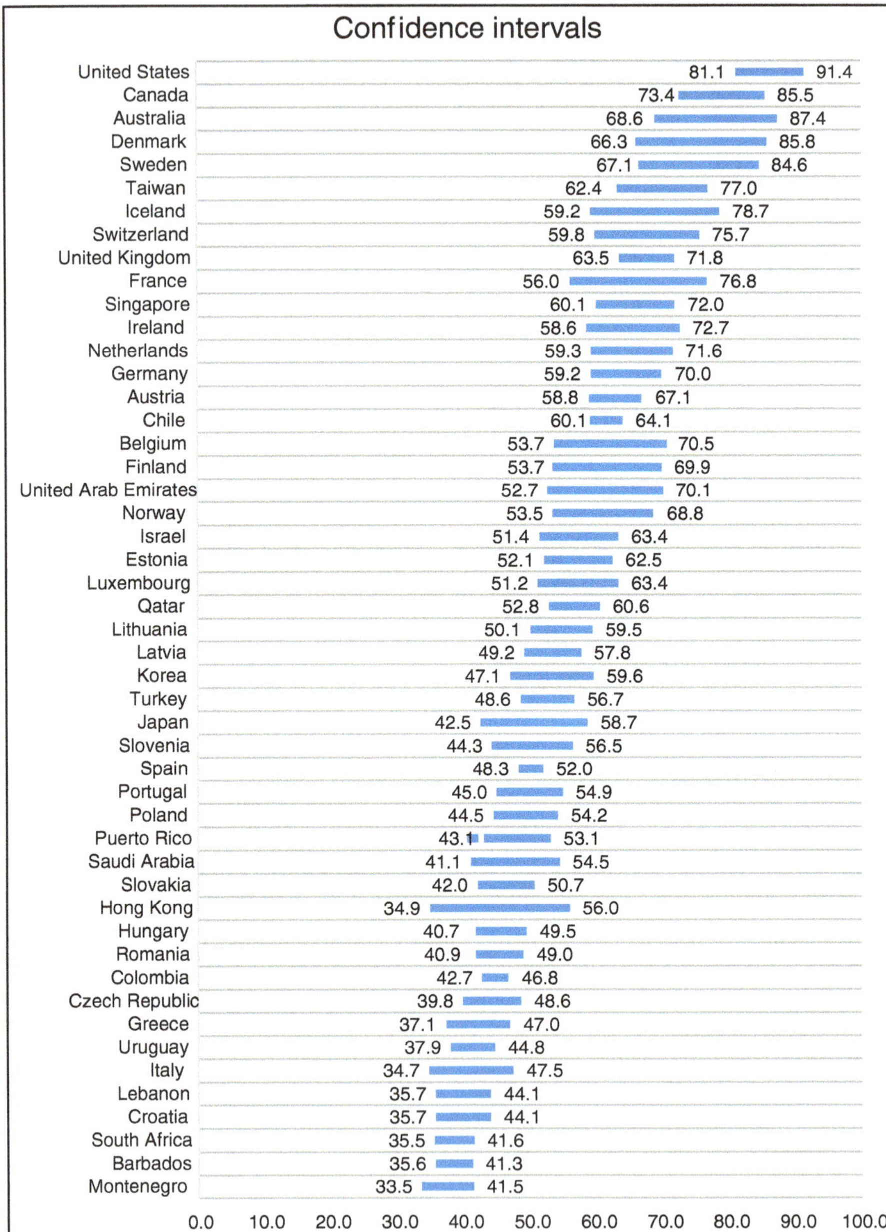

Table 3.1 (continued)

Czech Republic	39.8	48.6
Greece	37.1	47.0
Uruguay	37.9	44.8
Italy	34.7	47.5
Lebanon	35.7	44.1
Croatia	35.7	44.1
South Africa	35.5	41.6
Barbados	35.6	41.3
Montenegro	33.5	41.5
Malaysia	32.5	41.5
Macedonia	32.3	40.9
Costa Rica	33.3	39.1
Kazakhstan	31.5	39.2
China	33.0	36.9
Argentina	32.2	37.4
Tunisia	27.5	41.3
Jordan	29.0	37.9
Thailand	31.4	35.3
Botswana	31.4	34.7
Panama	30.3	34.5
Russia	27.9	36.5
Bolivia	30.1	34.2
Peru	30.4	33.7
Dominican Republic	28.6	34.7
Namibia	28.3	34.2
Serbia	24.4	37.4
Algeria	27.9	33.0
Belize	24.9	34.6
Morocco	26.0	33.0
Libya	25.4	32.3
Iran	27.1	30.5
Georgia	23.6	33.8
Bosnia and Herzegovina	25.7	31.5
Trinidad & Tobago	26.1	30.3
Vietnam	26.1	30.2
Nigeria	27.1	29.1
Mexico	26.0	29.3
Ecuador	26.2	28.6
Egypt	23.6	31.1
Jamaica	25.6	29.0
Philippines	25.3	28.6
Brazil	25.3	26.8
El Salvador	23.8	27.4
India	22.9	27.0
Ghana	23.4	25.6
Venezuela	21.5	26.6
Zambia	22.0	23.6
Indonesia	21.9	23.7
Guatemala	19.7	22.6
Pakistan	17.9	21.6
Suriname	16.2	22.4
Angola	17.5	19.7
Ethiopia	16.1	19.1
Cameroon	16.6	18.6
Uganda	15.1	16.5
Bangladesh	13.4	17.0
Burkina Faso	14.0	16.2
Malawi	11.8	13.0

3.5 The Ranking of the 3As

By definition, the GEI is a three-component index that takes into account the different aspects of the entrepreneurial ecosystem. However, all three components, called sub-indices, are in themselves complex measures that include various characteristics of entrepreneurial attitudes, entrepreneurial abilities, and entrepreneurial aspirations.

Entrepreneurial attitudes are societies' attitudes toward entrepreneurship, which we define as a population's general feelings about recognizing opportunities, knowing entrepreneurs personally, endowing entrepreneurs with high status, accepting the risks associated with business startups, and having the skills to launch a business successfully. The benchmark individuals are those who can recognize valuable business opportunities and have the skills to exploit them; who attach high status to entrepreneurs; who can bear and handle startup risks; who know other entrepreneurs personally (i.e., have a network or role models); and who can generate future entrepreneurial activities.

Moreover, these people can provide the cultural support, financial resources, and networking potential to those who are already entrepreneurs or want to start a business. Entrepreneurial attitudes are important because they express the general feeling of the population toward entrepreneurs and entrepreneurship. Countries need people who can recognize valuable business opportunities, and who perceive that they have the required skills to exploit these opportunities. Moreover, if national attitudes toward entrepreneurship are positive, it will generate cultural support, financial support, and networking benefits for those who want to start businesses.

Entrepreneurial abilities refer to the entrepreneurs' characteristics and those of their businesses. Different types of entrepreneurial abilities can be distinguished within the realm of new business efforts. Creating businesses may vary by industry sector, the legal form of organization, and demographics—age, education, etc. We define entrepreneurial abilities as startups in the medium- or high-technology sectors that are initiated by educated entrepreneurs, and launched because of someone being motivated by an opportunity in an environment that is not overly competitive. In order to calculate the opportunity startup rate, we use the GEM TEA Opportunity Index. TEA captures new startups not only as the creation of new ventures but also as startups within existing businesses, such as a spinoff or other entrepreneurial effort. Differences in the quality of startups are quantified by the entrepreneur's education level—that is, if they have a postsecondary education—and the uniqueness of the product or service as measured by the level of competition. Moreover, it is generally maintained that opportunity motivation is a sign of better planning, a more sophisticated strategy, and higher growth expectations than "necessity" motivation in startups.

Entrepreneurial aspiration reflects the quality aspects of startups and new businesses. Some people just hate their employer and want to be their own boss, while others want to create the next Microsoft. Entrepreneurial aspiration is defined as the early-stage entrepreneur's effort to introduce new products and/or services, develop

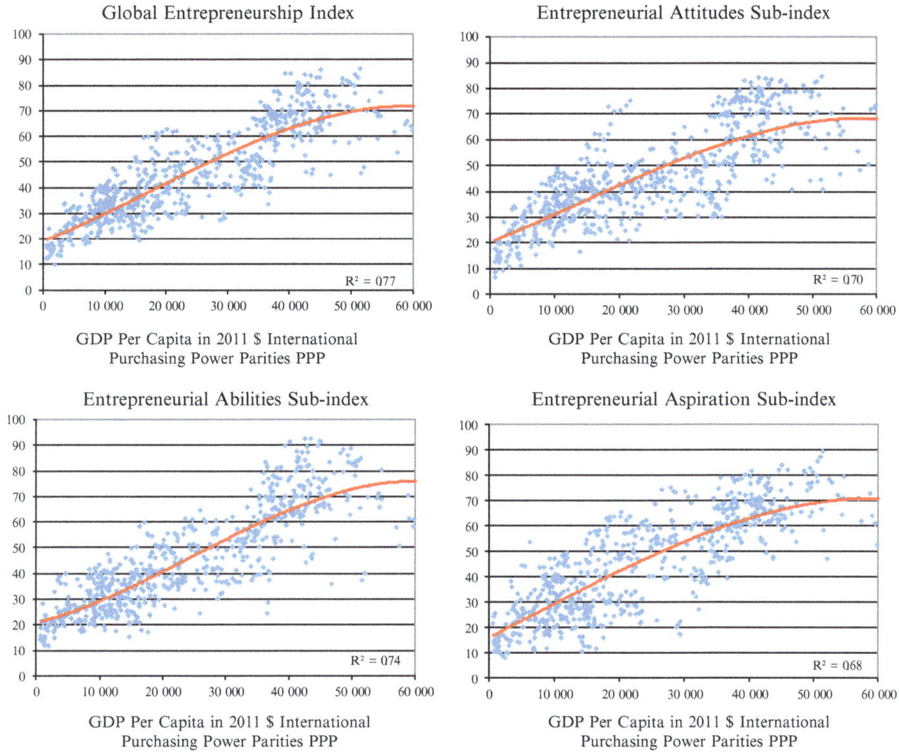

Fig. 3.2 The three sub-indices in terms of per capita real GDP (2002–2014, all data included) (Number of observations = 684)

new production processes, penetrate foreign markets, substantially increase their company's staff, and finance their business with formal and/or informal venture capital. Product and process innovation, internationalization, and high growth are considered the key characteristics of entrepreneurship. Here we added a finance variable to capture the informal and formal venture capital potential that is vital for innovative startups and high-growth firms.

Each of these three building blocks of entrepreneurship influences the other two. For example, entrepreneurial attitudes influence entrepreneurial abilities and entrepreneurial aspirations, while entrepreneurial aspirations and abilities also influence entrepreneurial attitudes.

Figure 3.2 shows the relationship between the GEI, the three sub-indices, and national per capita wealth, based on purchasing power parity GDP. In all the figures, we provide the associated trend line and R-squared values. All the trend lines are based on third-degree polynomial equations.

The overall Index shows a good fit and a positive relationship between development and entrepreneurship. The two move in the same direction, with an $R^2 = 0.77$, which implies a close, strong relationship between entrepreneurship and economic

Table 3.2 The Global Entrepreneurship Index and sub-index ranks of the first 25 countries, 2016

Country	GEI	GEI rank	ATT	ATT rank	ABT	ABT rank	ASP	ASP rank
United States	86.2	1	84.4	1	84.8	2	89.5	1
Canada	79.5	2	78.1	2	81.3	4	79.0	3
Australia	78.0	3	75.2	4	81.8	3	77.0	4
Denmark	76.0	4	71.1	8	87.1	1	69.9	10
Sweden	75.9	5	77.3	3	79.9	5	70.4	8
Taiwan	69.7	6	61.6	14	65.9	15	81.6	2
Iceland	68.9	7	70.2	10	69.8	10	66.8	13
Switzerland	67.8	8	63.4	13	68.9	11	71.0	6
United Kingdom	67.7	9	70.9	9	73.3	7	58.8	26
France	66.4	10	58.3	17	73.4	6	67.4	12
Singapore	66.0	11	49.2	32	71.8	8	76.9	5
Ireland	65.6	12	59.0	16	71.3	9	66.6	14
Netherlands	65.4	13	71.7	7	66.4	14	58.2	29
Germany	64.6	14	60.1	15	67.4	13	66.2	15
Austria	62.9	15	64.5	12	63.7	17	60.6	23
Chile	62.1	16	74.9	5	47.9	35	63.4	17
Belgium	62.1	17	53.4	24	62.4	18	70.4	9
Finland	61.8	18	72.1	6	52.5	26	60.7	22
United Arab Emirates	61.4	19	55.5	20	57.8	21	70.9	7
Norway	61.1	20	69.9	11	68.3	12	45.1	45
Israel	57.4	21	52.9	25	50.2	32	69.0	11
Estonia	57.3	22	56.5	18	57.2	22	58.3	27
Luxembourg	57.2	23	44.0	44	65.7	16	62.0	19
Qatar	56.7	24	53.8	23	51.4	28	64.9	16
Lithuania	54.8	25	47.9	34	58.2	19	58.2	28

development. Unlike other entrepreneurship measures that find an L-shaped (self-employment rate) or a U-shaped (Total Early-Phase Entrepreneurial Activity index) relationship between entrepreneurship and development, we find a mild S-shaped relationship.

The relationship between the Entrepreneurial Attitudes sub-index (ATT) and development is shown in the top right figure. The relationship is similar to the logarithmic function, implying that overall entrepreneurship attitudes increase as a country develops. The explanatory power, based on the $R^2 = 0.70$, shows a significant, strong correlation between ATT and per capita GDP.

The lower-left figure contains the Entrepreneurial Abilities sub-index (ABT) values in terms of economic development. The explanatory power, $R^2 = 0.74$, is the highest among the three sub-indices, implying a close and strong relationship between entrepreneurial abilities and development.

The trend of the Entrepreneurial Aspirations sub-index (ASP) is probably no surprise. The explanatory power of $R^2 = 0.68$ is significant and strong.

Table 3.2 shows the ranking of the first 25 countries in the GEI and the rank of the sub-index. The United States is 1st in the overall Index, and also in two out of the three sub-indices. Australia is 3rd in attitudes and aspirations, and 4th in abilities, as it is more interested in high-impact entrepreneurship than in replicative activities. Chile represents a more unbalanced case, ranking 15th in the overall Index, 16th in attitudes, 5th in abilities, and 34th in aspirations. This is a huge challenge for Chile and many other Latin American economies. Generally, countries that rank at the bottom of the GEI also rank at the bottom of the three sub-indices. Israel ranks 21st in the overall Index but performs poorly in attitudes and abilities. However, it ranks 11th in Aspirations, despite having poorer attitudes and abilities. For the "startup nation" it has an overall poor ranking in startup skills – at the bottom of the top 25 countries.

Tables 3.3, 3.4 and 3.5 list the ranks and the 14 pillar values of the first 25 countries for the three sub-indices. Each table gives the values for each of the pillars that make up the respective sub-index.

Table 3.3 Entrepreneurial attitudes sub-index and pillar values for the first 25 countries, 2016

Countries	ATT	Opportunity perception	Startup skills	Risk acceptance	Networking	Cultural support
United States	84.4	1.000	1.000	0.877	0.657	0.829
Canada	78.1	1.000	0.667	0.795	0.700	0.826
Sweden	77.3	1.000	0.609	0.761	0.962	0.855
Australia	75.2	0.890	0.879	0.685	0.641	0.738
Chile	74.9	1.000	1.000	0.745	0.827	0.762
Finland	72.1	0.631	0.721	0.735	1.000	0.931
Netherlands	71.7	0.729	0.735	0.764	0.876	1.000
Denmark	71.1	0.789	0.522	0.733	0.853	0.914
United Kingdom	70.9	0.772	0.602	0.787	0.747	0.830
Iceland	70.2	0.433	0.896	0.854	1.000	0.656
Norway	69.9	0.904	0.508	0.892	0.841	0.941
Austria	64.5	0.595	0.778	0.700	0.819	0.649
Switzerland	63.4	0.601	0.503	0.862	0.705	0.689
Taiwan	61.6	0.642	0.510	0.604	0.785	0.608
Germany	60.1	0.660	0.444	0.636	0.577	0.787
Ireland	59.0	0.332	0.737	0.694	0.728	0.725
France	58.3	0.508	0.412	0.691	0.780	0.648
Estonia	56.5	0.396	0.648	0.490	0.863	0.569
Saudi Arabia	56.5	1.000	0.789	0.240	0.776	0.646
United Arab Emirates	55.5	0.660	0.365	0.395	0.758	0.788
Spain	54.5	0.366	0.901	0.638	0.663	0.405
Bahrain	54.0	0.664	0.431	0.459	0.859	0.566
Qatar	53.8	0.970	0.142	0.631	0.817	0.916
Belgium	53.4	0.647	0.475	0.584	0.446	0.570
Israel	52.9	0.652	0.433	0.507	0.681	0.586

Pillar values are the normalized pillar scores after the average pillar correction.

Table 3.4 Entrepreneurial abilities sub-index and pillar values for the first 25 countries, 2016

Countries	ABT	Opportunity startup	Technology absorption	Human capital	Competition
Denmark	87.1	1.000	1.000	0.992	1.000
United States	84.8	0.775	0.808	0.917	0.992
Australia	81.8	0.946	0.874	0.887	0.673
Canada	81.3	0.799	0.678	0.979	0.881
Sweden	79.9	0.921	1.000	0.763	0.795
France	73.4	0.688	0.864	0.863	0.798
United Kingdom	73.3	0.906	0.681	0.765	0.768
Singapore	71.8	1.000	0.710	1.000	0.600
Ireland	71.3	0.628	0.808	0.989	0.853
Iceland	69.8	1.000	0.985	0.513	0.570
Switzerland	68.9	0.621	0.647	0.809	0.912
Norway	68.3	1.000	0.877	0.606	0.680
Germany	67.4	0.764	0.656	0.551	0.880
Netherlands	66.4	0.901	0.687	0.537	0.849
Taiwan	65.9	0.883	0.549	0.845	0.486
Luxembourg	65.7	0.585	0.957	0.986	1.000
Austria	63.7	0.643	0.826	0.455	0.909
Belgium	62.4	0.522	0.415	0.894	0.853
Lithuania	58.2	0.721	0.558	0.896	0.412
Japan	58.1	0.573	0.885	0.989	0.508
United Arab Emirates	57.8	0.634	0.359	1.000	0.534
Estonia	57.2	0.595	0.508	0.548	0.717
Puerto Rico	56.6	0.787	0.294	0.904	0.758
Latvia	55.3	0.633	0.614	0.603	0.519
Spain	52.6	0.455	0.705	0.462	0.603

Pillar values are the normalized pillar scores after the average pillar correction.

As stated earlier, entrepreneurial attitude is defined as the general attitude of a country's population toward recognizing opportunities, knowing entrepreneurs personally, attaching high status to entrepreneurs, accepting the risks associated with a business startup, and having the skills to successfully launch businesses. Entrepreneurial attitudes are important because they express the population's general feelings toward entrepreneurs and entrepreneurship.

The benchmark individuals are those who can (1) recognize valuable business opportunities, (2) have the necessary skills to exploit these opportunities, (3) attach high status to and respect entrepreneurs, (4) handle startup risk, and (5) know entrepreneurs personally (i.e., have a network or role models). Moreover, these people can provide the cultural support, financial resources, and networking potential to those who are already entrepreneurs or want to start a business. The United States leads the Entrepreneurial Attitudes sub-index, followed by Canada, Australia,

Table 3.5 Entrepreneurial aspirations sub-index and pillar values for the first 25 countries, 2016

Countries	ASP	Product innovation	Process innovation	High growth	Internationalization	Risk capital
United States	89.5	0.890	0.885	0.961	0.913	1.000
Taiwan	81.6	1.000	0.972	1.000	0.547	1.000
Canada	79.0	0.728	0.647	0.695	1.000	0.995
Australia	77.0	0.624	0.750	0.653	1.000	0.941
Singapore	76.9	0.707	1.000	1.000	1.000	0.821
Switzerland	71.0	0.880	0.745	0.403	0.941	1.000
United Arab Emirates	70.9	0.871	0.457	1.000	0.737	0.993
Sweden	70.4	0.837	1.000	0.478	0.780	0.652
Belgium	70.4	0.686	0.854	0.535	0.955	0.804
Denmark	69.9	1.000	0.714	0.653	0.449	0.974
Israel	69.0	1.000	1.000	0.598	0.599	0.941
France	67.4	0.682	0.871	0.575	0.709	0.766
Iceland	66.8	0.680	0.897	0.675	0.795	0.502
Ireland	66.6	0.751	0.681	0.848	0.795	0.634
Germany	66.2	0.698	0.756	0.606	0.634	0.764
Qatar	64.9	0.794	1.000	0.971	0.561	1.000
Chile	63.4	1.000	0.348	0.797	0.704	0.691
Turkey	62.1	0.789	0.422	1.000	0.430	0.796
Luxembourg	62.0	1.000	0.767	0.439	1.000	0.878
Korea	61.1	0.846	0.889	0.604	0.474	0.788
Japan	60.7	1.000	1.000	1.000	0.401	0.597
Finland	60.7	0.900	0.850	0.478	0.532	0.496
Austria	60.6	0.772	0.732	0.339	0.859	0.629
Poland	59.0	0.680	0.441	0.703	0.932	0.604
Slovakia	58.8	0.565	0.549	0.671	1.000	0.785

Pillar values are the normalized pillar scores after the average pillar correction.

Sweden, Finland, Chile, Norway, Iceland, the Netherlands, and United Kingdom. Chile's sixth place is a very strong showing for a South American country. Factor-driven African and Asian countries, including Swaziland, Mali, Sierra Leone, Ethiopia, Bangladesh, Pakistan, Malawi, Chad, and Burundi, are at the bottom.

High entrepreneurial abilities are associated with startups in the medium- or high-technology sectors that are initiated by educated entrepreneurs and launched because of opportunity motivation in a not too competitive environment. Quality differences in startups are quantified by the motivation and education level of the entrepreneur, and by the uniqueness of the product or service, as measured by the level of competition.

Denmark ranks number one on the Entrepreneurial Abilities sub-index and has a very strong showing in three of the four pillars, including Human Capital, Technology Absorption, and Competition. The US ranks second and is relatively weak in Opportunity Startup and Technology Absorption. Australia is stronger than the US in two pillars, Opportunity Startups and Technology Absorption, but weaker in Human Capital and very weak in Competition. Canada ranks fourth, with a significantly lower Entrepreneurial Abilities score than the United States and Australia. Canada is relatively strong in Human Capital but weak on Competition, which implies that fresh entrepreneurs are mainly looking for market niches that do not have many competitors. The high-share startups are initiated in the medium- and high-technology sectors, which is also a strong point for Canada. The first four countries are followed by the Sweden, France, the UK, Singapore, Ireland, and Iceland.

Entrepreneurial aspiration is the early-stage entrepreneur's effort to introduce new products and/or services, develop new production processes, penetrate foreign markets, substantially increase the firm's staff, and finance a business with formal and/or informal venture capital. In other words, the effort to start new companies that will generate wealth and can be scaled. Product and process innovation, internationalization, and high growth are considered characteristics of entrepreneurship. The benchmark entrepreneurs are those whose businesses (1) produce and sell products/services considered to be new to at least some customers, (2) use a technology less than 5 years old, (3) have sales in foreign markets, (4) plan to employ at least ten people, and (5) have greater than 50 percent growth over the next 5 years. The Finance variable captures the informal venture capital potential, as well as the development of capital, venture capital, and credit markets, which is vital for innovative startups and high-growth firms.

Like the two other sub-indices, the United States leads in the Entrepreneurial Aspirations sub-index. While showing some weakness in Internationalization, it is very strong in Risk Capital and Process Innovation. Taiwan is second, with a strong showing in High Growth and Product Innovation, followed by Canada, Australia, Singapore, Switzerland, the UAE, and, which round out the top ten. The surprise is Israel falling out of the top ten in Aspirations, with a very weak showing in High Growth and Internationalization but with a very strong performance in Product and Process Innovation.

3.6 Summaries and Conclusion

Entrepreneurship is similar to other social creatures, in that it is a multidimensional phenomenon whose exact meaning is difficult to identify. There is only one thing more difficult: how to measure this vaguely defined creature. Over the decades, researchers have created several entrepreneurship indicators, but none has been able to reflect the complex nature of entrepreneurship and provide a plausible explanation of its role in development. The Global Entrepreneurship Index is the first, and presently the only, complex measure of the national-level entrepreneurship ecosystem that reflects the multifaceted nature of entrepreneurship. In this chapter, we presented the entrepreneurial performance of 132 of the world's countries, which included country-level values for the GEI—entrepreneurial attitudes, entrepreneurial abilities, and entrepreneurial aspirations—and for the 14 pillars.

While the GEI represents the contextual features of entrepreneurship, it is also possible to analyze changes in entrepreneurship and its components in terms of development. We presented the relationship between Index values and development, as measured by per capita GDP. While previous studies found that entrepreneurship, measured primarily in terms of activities, has a U- or L-shaped relationship with national per capita income, we noticed a linear, mildly S-shaped relationship, which indicates that entrepreneurship is more prevalent in richer countries. This finding fits more accurately with our present knowledge of the nature of the entrepreneurial ecosystem than U- or L-shaped relationships between the variables. The final ranking, with Nordic and Anglo-Saxon countries at the top and developing countries at the bottom, also reflects what we expect development trends to look like.

In the final part of the chapter, we compared certain factors between some important countries and country groups. The pillar-level analysis provides a proper tool for showing the real differences and variations in entrepreneurship, which is found to vary substantially not only across countries with different levels of development but also among countries with similar per capita GDP. The United States is the leading entrepreneurial country: despite a minimal decline in its GEI score, the United States is still number one not only in the GEI but also in two of three sub-indices. While the leading countries have similar entrepreneurial features, European nations and the European Union lag behind the United States, and this gap is widening. It is particularly evident in the PIIGS (Portugal, Italy, Ireland, Greece and Spain), which lag far behind the larger EU countries and the Nordic fringe. Latin America will also require a substantial increase in entrepreneurship to reach levels comparable to those of North America. Comparing the developing countries shows that the configuration of the 14 pillars is similar in shape but at different levels across the three main regions of the world. A detailed examination of entrepreneurship and the change in its components over the phases of development is the focus of the following chapter.

References

Acemoglu, D., & Johnson, S. (2005). Unbundling institutions. *Journal of Political Economy, 113*, 949–995.

Acs, Z. J. (2010). Entrepreneurship and economic development: The Valley of Backwardness. *Annals of Innovation & Entrepreneurship, 1*, 1–18.

Acs, Z. J., Braunerhjelm, P., Audretsch, D. B., & Carlsson, B. (2009). The knowledge spillover theory of entrepreneurship. *Small Business Economics, 32*(1), 15–30.

Acs, Z. J., Parsons, W., & Tracy, S. (2008). *High impact firms: Gazelles revisited* (Office of Advocacy working paper, U.S. Small Business Administration). http://www.sba.gov/advocacy/847/17231

Acs, Z. J., & Varga, A. (2005). Entrepreneurship, agglomeration and technological change. *Small Business Economics, 24*, 323–334.

Acs, Z. J., & Virgil, N. (2011). Entrepreneurship and economic development. *Foundations and Trends in Entrepreneurship, 6*(1), 1–68.

Bates, T. (1990). Entrepreneur human capital inputs and small business longevity. *The Review of Economics and Statistics, 72*, 551–559.
Baumol, W. (1990). Entrepreneurship: Productive, unproductive and destructive. *Journal of Political Economy, 98*, 893–921.
Baumol, W., Litan, R., & Schramm, C. (2007). *Good capitalism, bad capitalism, and the economics of growth and prosperity*. New Haven, CT: Yale University Press.
Banerjee, A. V., & Duflo, E. (2012). *Poor economics: A radical rethinking of the way to fight global poverty*. New York: Public Affairs.
Bhola, R., Verheul, I., Thurik, R., & Grilo, I. (2006). *Explaining engagement levels of opportunity and necessity entrepreneurs (EIM working paper series H200610)*. Zoetermeer: EIM.
Caliendo, M., Fossen, F. M., & Kritikos, A. S. (2009). Risk attitudes of nascent entrepreneurs: New evidence from an experimentally validated survey. *Small Business Economics, 32*, 153–167.
Coad, A., & Rao, R. (2008). Innovation and firm growth in "complex technology" sectors: A quantile regression approach. *Research Policy, 37*, 633–648.
Davidsson, P. (2004). *Researching entrepreneurship*. New York: Springer.
De Clercq, D., Sapienza, H. J., & Crijns, H. (2005). The internationalization of small and medium firms. *Small Business Economics, 24*, 409–419.
Easterly, W. (2001). The lost decade: Developing countries' stagnation in spite of policy reform 1980–1998. *Journal of Economic Growth, 6*, 141–143.
Gartner, W. B. (1990). What are we talking about when we talk about entrepreneurship? *Journal of Business Venturing, 5*(1), 15–28.
Gompers, P., & Lerner, J. (2004). *The venture capital cycle*. Cambridge, MA: MIT Press.
Groh, A., Liechtenstein, H., & Lieser, K. (2012). The global venture capital and private equity country attractiveness index, 2012.
Guiso, L., Sapienza, P., & Zingales, L. (2006). *Does culture affect economic outcomes?* (CEPR discussion paper no. 5505). http://ssrn.com/abstract=905320
Ketkar, S., & Acs, Z. J. (2013). Where angels fear to tread. *Journal of International Entrepreneurship, 11*, 201–219.
Leibenstein, H. (1968). Entrepreneurship and development. *American Economic Review, 38*(2), 72–83.
Papagiannidis, S., & Li, F. (2005). Skills brokerage: A new model for business startups in the networked economy. *European Management Journal, 23*, 471–482.
Porter, M., Sachs, J., & McArthur, J. (2002). Executive summary: Competitiveness and stages of economic development. In M. Porter, J. Sachs, P. K. Cornelius, J. McArthur, & K. Schwab (Eds.), *The global competitiveness report 2001–2002* (pp. 16–25). New York: Oxford University Press.
Rostow, W. W. (1960). *The stages of economic growth: A non-communist manifesto*. Cambridge, UK: Cambridge University Press.
Sachs, J. (2005). *The end of poverty: Economic possibilities for our time*. New York: Penguin Press.
Shane, S., & Cable, D. (2003). Network ties, reputation, and the financing of new ventures. *Management Science, 48*, 364–381.
Stam, E., & Wennberg, K. (2009). The roles of R&D in new firm growth. *Small Business Economics, 33*(1), 77–89.
Wennekers, S., & Thurik, R. (1999). Linking entrepreneurship to economic growth. *Small Business Economics, 13*(1), 27–55.
Woolridge, A. (2009, March 14). Global heroes: A special report on entrepreneurship. *The Economist*, 1–19.

Chapter 4
Country and Country Group Performance

In this section, we compare the entrepreneurial performance of countries within regions. As we have already seen, the entrepreneurial performance of countries can vary widely across the world. This is because, for example, countries in different stages of development may exhibit similar features, whereas differences across stages of development are usually larger. The significant differences between stages of economic development mean that not much can be learned by comparing a rich country like the United States to a poor country such as Zambia because the economic conditions in these two countries are so different. It makes much more sense to compare countries to similar nations, as this allows meaningful comparisons and helps us make better sense of the patterns we see in the data.

We have grouped the 132 countries into six groups according to their location and level of development (Table 4.1). We analyze the entrepreneurial performance of different country groups as compared to the world average (the unweighted average of the 132 countries for each of the GEI pillars). In addition, we take a close look at three countries in each country group: one at the top, one at the middle, and one at the bottom of the regional ranking.

Table 4.1 presents the countries assigned in each country group.

4.1 Sub-Saharan Africa

Africa is the second largest continent by area and the largest if measured by number of countries. Africa's individual countries and economies exhibit considerable heterogeneity, with significant cultural and economic differences between the North and the South, and between the East and the West.

In this analysis, we look at Sub-Saharan African countries. North African countries are analyzed as part of the Middle East and North Africa Region. As we can see in Table 4.2, this group includes some of the least developed countries. This is reflected in the countries' global GEI rankings and GEI scores. The leading country

Z. Acs et al., *Global Entrepreneurship and Development Index 2016*,
SpringerBriefs in Economics, DOI 10.1007/978-3-319-63844-7_4

Table 4.1 Country groups analyzed in this chapter

Asia-Pacific	Europe		Middle East/ North Africa	North America	South and Central America/Caribbean	Sub-Saharan Africa
Australia	Albania	Luxembourg	Algeria	Canada	Argentina	Angola
Bangladesh	Austria	Macedonia	Bahrain	Mexico	Barbados	Benin
Brunei	Belgium	Moldova	Egypt	United States	Belize	Botswana
Darussal am	Bosnia and	Montenegro	Iran		Bolivia	Burkina Faso
Cambodia	Herzegovina	Netherlands	Israel		Brazil	Burundi
China	Bulgaria	Norway	Jordan		Chile	Cameroon
Hong Kong	Croatia	Poland	Kuwait		Colombia	Chad
India	Cyprus	Portugal	Lebanon		Costa Rica	Côte d'Ivoire
Indonesia	Czech Republic	Romania	Libya		Dominican Republic	Ethiopia
Japan	Denmark	Russia	Morocco		Ecuador	Gabon
Kazakhstan	Estonia	Serbia	Oman		El Salvador	Gambia
Korea	Finland	Slovakia	Qatar		Guatemala	Ghana
Lao PDR	France	Slovenia	Saudi Arabia		Guyana	Kenya
Malaysia	Georgia	Spain	Tunisia		Honduras	Liberia
Myanmar	Germany	Sweden	United Arab		Jamaica	Madagascar
Pakistan	Greece	Switzerland	Emirates		Nicaragua	Malawi
Philippines	Hungary	Turkey			Panama	Mali
Singapore	Iceland	Ukraine			Paraguay	Mauritania
Sri Lanka	Ireland	United Kingdom			Peru	Mozambique
Taiwan	Italy				Puerto Rico	Namibia
Thailand	Latvia				Suriname	Nigeria
Vietnam	Lithuania				Trinidad & Tobago	Rwanda
					Uruguay	Senegal
					Venezuela	Sierra Leone
						South Africa
						Swaziland
						Tanzania
						Uganda
						Zambia

Table 4.2 GEI ranking of the Sub-Saharan African countries

GEI rank	Country	ATT	ABT	ASP	GEI
52	South Africa	34.4	37.0	44.0	38.5
66	Botswana	36.4	34.4	28.4	33.1
73	Namibia	30.2	27.9	35.6	31.3
85	Nigeria	32.4	26.7	25.1	28.1
86	Gabon	23.8	28.8	30.9	27.8
95	Swaziland	19.7	24.6	33.0	25.8
99	Ghana	33.5	22.4	17.8	24.5
102	Zambia	22.2	25.1	21.1	22.8
104	Kenya	23.3	21.8	21.2	22.1
106	Senegal	28.2	19.9	16.9	21.7
112	Angola	19.2	17.4	19.1	18.6
113	Rwanda	19.5	23.4	12.0	18.3
114	Ethiopia	13.8	23.5	15.5	17.6
115	Cameroon	20.2	16.9	15.6	17.6
116	Mozambique	16.5	21.0	15.2	17.6
118	Gambia. The	16.1	21.6	14.5	17.4
119	Liberia	17.5	21.2	13.4	17.3
120	Côte d'Ivoire	18.9	19.3	12.7	17.0
121	Tanzania	16.5	17.5	16.5	16.8
122	Mali	14.1	19.3	16.4	16.6
123	Uganda	21.1	14.5	11.8	15.8
124	Benin	19.6	17.6	10.2	15.8
126	Burkina Faso	13.4	19.1	12.8	15.1
127	Madagascar	12.3	21.3	10.2	14.6
128	Sierra Leone	13.5	18.0	11.5	14.3
129	Mauritania	15.3	14.6	9.6	13.2
130	Malawi	8.3	14.1	14.7	12.4
131	Burundi	6.4	18.6	10.6	11.9
132	Chad	9.0	11.6	9.0	9.9
	Sub-Saharan Africa	19.8	21.3	18.1	19.8

in this region, South Africa, achieves a GEI score of 38.5, which ranks it 52nd among the 132 countries analyzed in the global GEI ranking. South Africa is also the only Sub-Saharan country that ranks within the top 50 percent of the GEI countries. At the bottom we see Chad, whose GEI score of 9.9 ranks it second to last among the GEI countries. A total of 22 out of the 29 Sub-Saharan countries are found in the bottom quartile of the global GEI ranking.

Generally speaking, there is not much difference in the average performance of the region's sub-indices, with Aspirations posting the lowest average score at 18.1 and Abilities posting the highest average score at 21.3. However, even at this low level of development, there are important differences between Attitudes, Abilities, and Aspirations within individual Sub-Saharan countries. For example, Burundi's

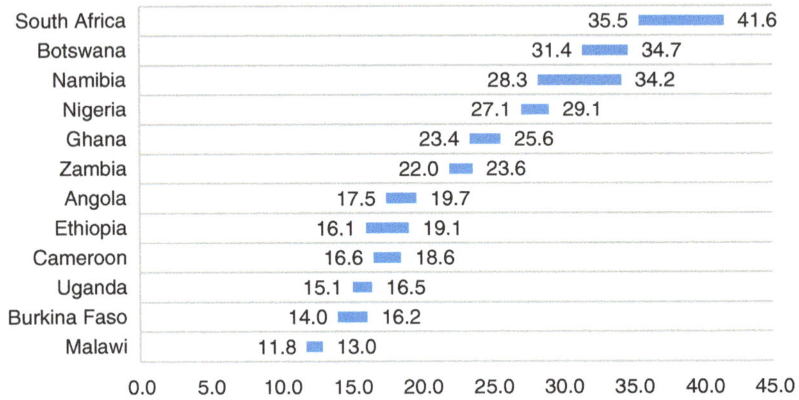

Fig. 4.1 Confidence intervals for Sub-Saharan African countries (**Countries with estimated individual data are not shown, as confidence intervals for these countries cannot be calculated)

score for Abilities (18.6) is almost three times as high as its score for Attitudes (6.4). Ghana's Attitudes score (33.5) is almost twice as high as its score for Aspirations (17.8). Madagascar's score for Abilities (21.3) is more than twice as high as its score for Aspirations (10.2). Thus, while the region has much catching up to do in all areas, different countries face distinctly different challenges (Fig. 4.1).

Table 4.2 confirms that, despite encouraging progress in recent years, Africa remains the least developed continent. This is also reflected in the analysis of individual GEI pillars, as shown in Fig. 4.2. With all countries combined, the African continent ranks below the world average for all pillars. Africa comes closest to the world average in Opportunity Perception, echoing the encouraging economic progress we have seen in the region in recent years. Other encouraging pillars are Opportunity Startup and Competition.

Because regional groups combine many countries, the resulting regional profiles tend to be more or less round. This mostly holds for Sub-Saharan Africa, too, with some notable exceptions. First, Sub-Saharan Africa seems to suffer from a clear bottleneck in Startup Skills. On the surface, this might appear inconsistent with the fact that Sub-Saharan African countries exhibit some of the highest self-employment rates in the world, but it is actually indicative of a quality problem, as most African self-employment is of low quality. While starting a necessity-driven self-employment activity is easy (e.g., setting up a fruit stand on a street corner), building a sophisticated startup is difficult. Education is required for more sophisticated activities. This is Africa's handicap, as its gross enrollment in tertiary education (the institutional component of the startup skills pillar) is the lowest of all regions.

Other notable African weaknesses are found in Attitudes: the normalized values of Human Capital, Risk Capital, Process Innovation, and Risk Acceptance are all at or below 0.20. On the other hand, there has been notable improvement in Opportunity Perception and Cultural Support over last year. Whereas Opportunity Perception counted among regional bottlenecks in 2015, this year it is the region's stand-out strength.

Fig. 4.2 Pillar-level comparison between Sub-Saharan Africa and the world average

Overall, entrepreneurship in Africa is held back by institutional factors—a pattern typical of developing countries. Of all the regions analyzed, Sub-Saharan Africa's mean score for institutional factors is the lowest, at 0.38. This compares to individual-level factors, for which Sub-Saharan Africa scores 0.58, more or less on par with other regions. Thus, to better exploit its entrepreneurial potential, Sub-Saharan African countries need to improve their institutional conditions for entrepreneurship.

In Fig. 4.3 we compare the profiles of three Sub-Saharan African countries. South Africa is the best all-round performer in Sub-Saharan Africa in entrepreneurship. Angola is in the middle group, ranking 11th among the 29 countries. Uganda stands at 21st among the Sub-Saharan countries, as it is gradually recovering from recent instability.

We see that the profiles of the three countries are quite different. South Africa clearly stands apart from Angola and Uganda for some of its Abilities variables (notably, Competition and Opportunity Startup) and many of its Aspirations variables (notably, Product Innovation, Process Innovation, High Growth, and Internationalization). This signals that better institutions should create conditions in

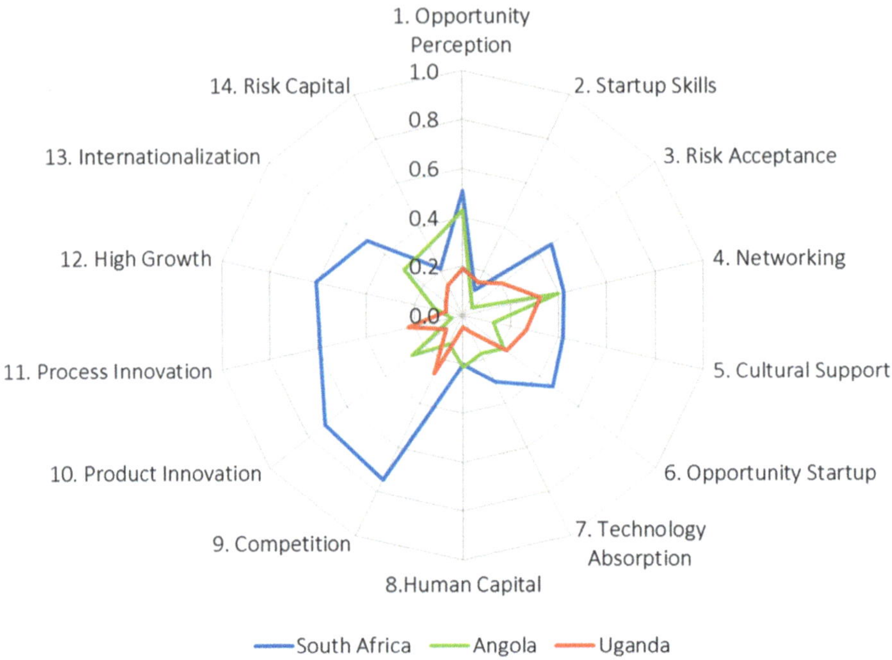

Fig. 4.3 Pillar-level comparison of South Africa, Angola, and Uganda

which aspirational entrepreneurial activity can flourish. On the other hand, South Africa is on par with Uganda for Startup Skills and with Angola for Opportunity Perception, Networking, and Human Capital.

For Angola, the strongest aspects are Opportunity Perception and Networking. However, it is held back by generally poor Aspirations and some Attitudes, notably, Risk Acceptance, Startup Skills, and Cultural Support. The low level of Risk Acceptance probably reflects a high level of corruption and poor enforcement of contracts.

Uganda is near the bottom of the Sub-Saharan African countries. Although it enjoys relative bright spots in Networking, Cultural Support, and Competition, Uganda needs to do considerable work to improve its institutions and reinforce internal stability, both of which currently hold back its entrepreneurial potential.

The profiles are highly uneven for all three countries—a pattern typical of developing economies. The uneven profiles suggest the existence of bottlenecks that hold back the countries' entrepreneurial performance. While even the leading country in the region faces significant individual bottlenecks, the positive news is that, by focusing on alleviating bottlenecks, these countries could achieve significant progress relative to the effort they expend. This contrasts with countries with rounder profiles, because in such countries the opportunities for quick wins tend to be fewer.

4.2 Middle East and North Africa (MENA)

The MENA region comprises 15 countries in Middle East and North Africa (Table 4.3). This region also exhibits a high-level of diversity. On the one end of the wealth scale are some of the richest countries in the world (as measured by GDP per capita), the oil-rich Persian Gulf economies. This region also includes several lower-income economies, some of which continue to experience turmoil from the events of the Arab Spring. This region is considerably more developed than Sub-Saharan Africa, with double the regional mean GEI score, and most of its countries are in the top 50 percent of the global GEI ranking (except for Algeria, Morocco, Libya, Iran, and Egypt). The three sub-indices are quite evenly balanced; the highest mean score is observed for Attitudes, but the Aspirations and Abilities mean scores are almost at the same level. The leading entrepreneurial economy in this group is the United Arab Emirates, followed closely by Israel and Qatar. The lowest GEI scores are observed for Algeria, Morocco, Libya, Iran, and Egypt. The common feature shared by this bottom group of MENA countries is fairly illiberal and controlled economies, where market access is often monopolized by a ruling business elite (Fig. 4.4).

The most notable phenomenon affecting this region in recent years was the Arab Spring, the wave of popular revolutions that saw some of the region's autocrats thrown out of power—most spectacularly in Tunisia, Libya, and Egypt. In some countries, such as Bahrain, the ruling families have successfully resisted the popular uprisings, whereas the upheaval in Syria led to a violent civil conflict that threatens to undermine the stability of the entire region.

Table 4.3 GEI ranking of the Middle East and North African countries

GEI rank	Country	ATT	ABT	ASP	GEI
19	United Arab Emirates	55.5	57.8	70.9	61.4
21	Israel	52.9	50.2	69.0	57.4
24	Qatar	53.8	51.4	64.9	56.7
29	Bahrain	54.0	50.2	52.9	52.4
36	Saudi Arabia	56.5	40.0	46.8	47.8
38	Oman	44.4	44.1	49.1	45.9
39	Kuwait	51.6	39.5	45.7	45.6
50	Lebanon	50.9	33.9	34.9	39.9
62	Tunisia	38.7	34.6	30.0	34.4
64	Jordan	42.3	24.1	34.0	33.5
75	Algeria	34.9	29.5	27.0	30.5
78	Morocco	39.3	21.2	27.9	29.5
79	Libya	26.9	34.5	25.2	28.9
80	Iran	32.8	29.0	24.6	28.8
89	Egypt	35.2	17.9	28.9	27.3
	Middle East/North Africa	44.65	37.19	42.13	41.32

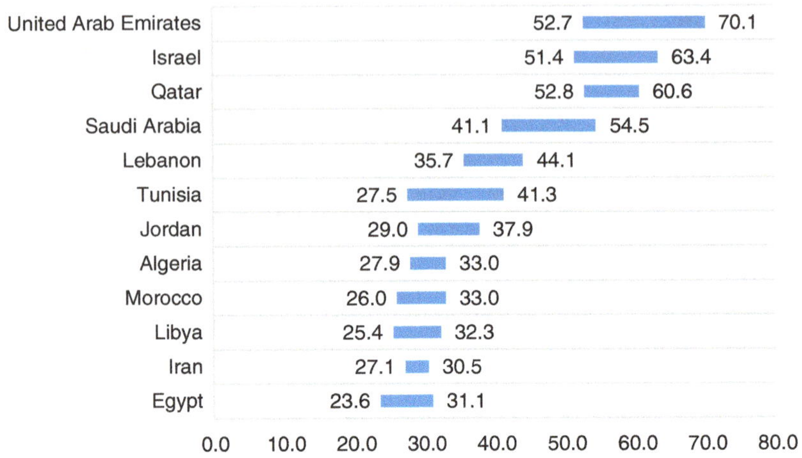

Fig. 4.4 Confidence intervals for the MENA countries (**Countries with estimated individual data are not shown, as confidence intervals for these countries cannot be calculated)

The Arab Spring phenomenon is noteworthy for our analysis because it emerged as a reaction against the ruling elites' monopolization of opportunity in a number of countries in the MENA region. The wave of upheavals was memorably started by the self-immolation of a street vendor in Tunisia, who was harassed by corrupt officials. In many countries, including Tunisia, Libya, and Egypt, the economies had become virtual private fiefdoms of the ruling elite, who monopolized entire economic sectors to the exclusion of the majority of the population. While much has been said about the democratic aspirations that were clearly an important motivation for the upheavals, it is useful to remember that the spark that ignited the Arab Spring had more to do with exclusion from opportunity than a deficit of democracy.

In terms of the GEI pillars, the MENA region as a whole performs close to the world average (Fig. 4.5). Most pillar values are almost exactly at the world average or very close to it. The differences are found in Opportunity Perception, Risk Capital, High Growth, and Networking, where the MENA countries collectively perform better than the world average.

We next look at three countries that illustrate different categories within this region. The oil-rich United Arab Emirates is one of the world's wealthiest countries in terms of GDP per capita. Algeria offers an example of the North African economies. Israel is a regional high-tech hub in the MENA region.

In Fig. 4.6 we see that the UAE is the top performer in the MENA region and a top performer globally for many pillars—notably, Human Capital, Risk Capital, and High Growth. For these pillars, the UAE's performance is a perfect 1, which reflects its financial wealth and also its high-quality human capital. The UAE's position as an important trading hub undoubtedly contributes to a high level of High Growth and Internationalization Aspirations in this country. Overall, the UAE exhibits a high level of Aspirations and a medium level of Attitudes and Abilities. The UAE's bottlenecks relate to Startup Skills, Technology Absorption, and Risk Acceptance,

Fig. 4.5 Pillar-level comparison of MENA region and the world

suggesting that an investment in entrepreneurship training and research capacity could bring about further improvements in the UAE's entrepreneurial performance. Given the UAE's uneven overall profile, these improvements could be quite substantial.

Algeria's profile is quite different from the UAE's. Algeria ranks 11th among the 15 countries in the MENA region and 75th globally. Its GEI score, 30.5, is less than half of that of the UAE's. Algeria's relative strengths are found in Opportunity Perception and Risk Capital, whereas monopolization of opportunity may be holding back the development of Abilities and Aspirations pillars.

Israel is another leader in the MENA region, and its GEI score of 57.1 ranks it 21st globally. Given Israel's global reputation for high-technology startup activity and its success in the NASDAQ listings, one may wonder why Israel is not ranked at the top of the MENA region. One answer to this question undoubtedly lies in the fact that Israel has quite a large sub-population that is economically inactive—namely, Orthodox Jews. This lowers Israel's overall score. As such, Israel exhibits (consistent with its reputation) notable strengths in Aspirations, whereas Attitudes

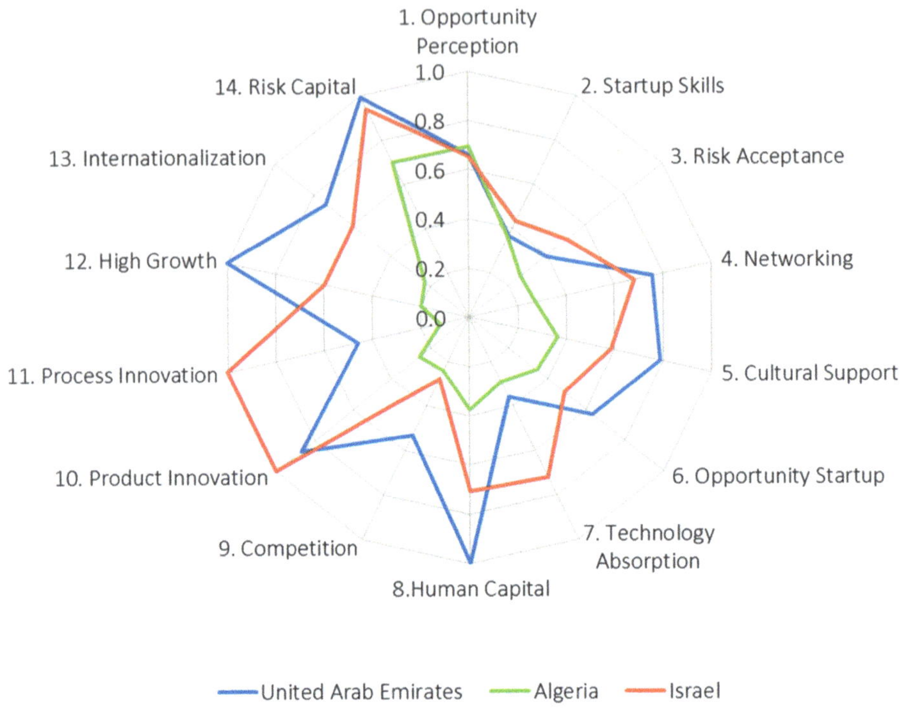

Fig. 4.6 Pillar-level comparison of the United Arab Emirates, Algeria, and Israel

and Abilities are quite even. Israel's strongest pillars are Innovation (both Product and Process) and Human Capital. Israel also shows strengths in Risk Capital and to some degree in High Growth and Internationalization. Israel's biggest bottlenecks are found in Competition, Startup Skills, and Opportunity Startup.

4.3 Asia-Pacific

The Asia-Pacific region offers some of the greatest potential for economic growth analyzed here, as it contains the developing economic behemoths of China and India, a number of emerging economies such as Turkey, Malaysia, Thailand, Vietnam, and Indonesia, and well-established and mature economies such as Australia, Japan, Korea, and Singapore (Table 4.4). On the other hand, this region also includes some of the poorest countries in the world, such as Cambodia, Myanmar, Laos, and Bangladesh. The economic potential of this region lies with its large and overall quite young population, notably in the developing Asian economies (Fig. 4.7).

When the profiles of the Asia-Pacific countries are combined, the result is a relatively round profile of pillar scores that does not differ much from the world average

Table 4.4 GEI ranking of the Asia-Pacific countries

GEI rank	Country	ATT	ABT	ASP	GEI
3	Australia	75.2	81.8	77.0	78.0
6	Taiwan	61.6	65.9	81.6	69.7
11	Singapore	49.2	71.8	76.9	66.0
27	Korea	47.2	51.8	61.1	53.4
30	Japan	33.0	58.1	60.7	50.6
40	Hong Kong	40.8	37.4	58.1	45.4
55	Brunei Darussalam	32.1	47.6	32.1	37.3
56	Malaysia	40.0	42.9	28.1	37.0
59	Kazakhstan	37.5	34.6	34.0	35.4
60	China	34.8	25.7	44.3	34.9
65	Thailand	35.4	37.5	27.3	33.4
84	Vietnam	26.3	30.7	27.5	28.2
91	Philippines	32.2	25.7	23.0	27.0
94	Lao PDR	13.7	40.0	24.0	25.9
97	Sri Lanka	19.8	28.0	28.6	25.5
98	India	23.2	24.3	27.4	24.9
101	Cambodia	10.6	32.7	25.6	23.0
103	Indonesia	28.8	22.8	16.7	22.8
109	Pakistan	15.6	19.2	24.5	19.8
117	Myanmar	11.0	24.7	16.8	17.5
125	Bangladesh	14.6	21.0	10.0	15.2
	Asia-Pacific	32.5	39.2	38.3	36.7

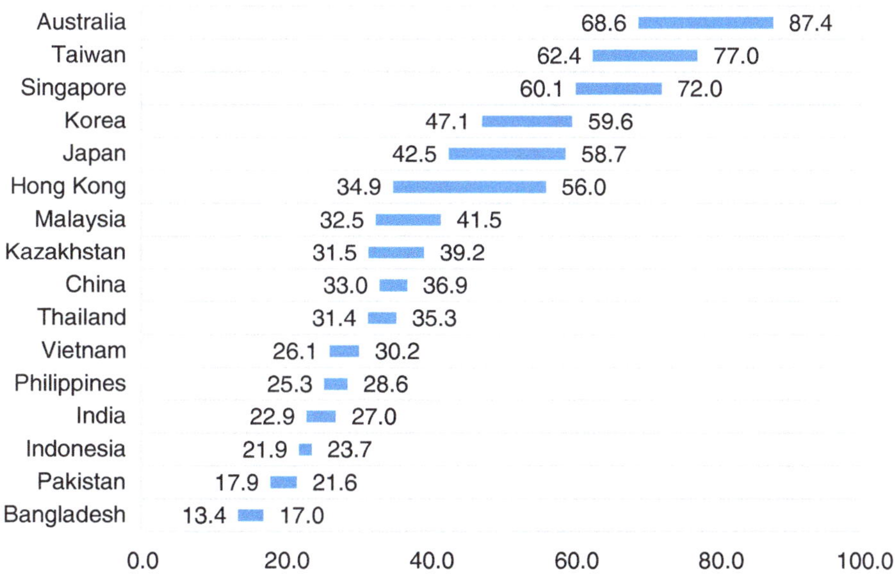

Fig. 4.7 Confidence intervals for Asia-Pacific countries (**Countries with estimated individual data are not shown, as confidence intervals for these countries cannot be calculated)

Fig. 4.8 Pillar-level comparison of Asia and the world

(Fig. 4.8). However, this even pattern hides the fact that some countries in this group are global top performers, while others are global laggards.

The striking feature in this region is its diversity in terms of economic and entrepreneurship development. On the one hand, the region contains some of the world's leading entrepreneurial economies such as Australia (3rd globally), Taiwan (6th), and Singapore (11th). On the other hand, the region also contains global laggards such as Myanmar (117th), Indonesia (103th), Pakistan (109th), and Bangladesh (125th). Interestingly, Korea and Japan do not rank at the top (4th and 5th in the region and 27th and 30th globally). This signals that the bulk of the innovative energy in these two countries is channeled through large, world-leading corporations. Even though both economies exhibit strong supply chains that include an important number of small- and medium-sized businesses, many of these (relative to the countries' innovative potential) content themselves with servicing local supply chains instead of seeking rapid global growth.

An interesting contrast is also observed between China and India. China's GEI score is almost 50 percent higher than India's, possibly suggesting that the bureaucratic red tape common in India constrains entrepreneurial activity in the country. This problem is common to all of the bottom-six countries in the Asia-Pacific group (i.e., India, Cambodia, Indonesia, Pakistan, Myanmar, and Bangladesh).

The Asia-Pacific region's weakest aspect is Attitudes toward entrepreneurship, whereas Abilities and Aspirations are almost at the same level with one another. However, there is great internal variance within the region: Australia's Attitudes score stands at 75.2, whereas Cambodia's Attitudes score, 10.6, is among the lowest in the global GEI ranking. There is similar variance across other sub-indices; for example, Aspirations scores range from Taiwan's high of 81.6 to Bangladesh's low of 10.0. Given this diversity, it makes sense to take a separate look at developing and mature Asia-Pacific economies, respectively.

The developing Asian countries represent the second least developed group, after Africa. The big challenge for these countries appears to be continuing to enhance institutional and regulatory conditions for entrepreneurship. For some countries, such as China, this inevitably will also mean gradual democratic liberalization to accommodate the desires of the growing middle class. For other countries, such as India and Pakistan, this means reducing red tape and strengthening the rule of law to enable ambitious entrepreneurship to flourish. For the emerging economies—notably, Malaysia and Thailand—this means strengthening the infrastructure for ambitious entrepreneurship and facilitating competitive market entry in the face of dominant industrial conglomerates. For the weakest economies, such as Cambodia, Laos, and Bangladesh, this means strengthening the institutional foundations for entrepreneurial activity and gradually developing human capital and physical infrastructure. Overall, there appears to be good potential for development, as many developing Asian countries have stable governance structures capable of channeling resources to facilitate desired policy developments.

The mature Asia-Pacific countries include some of the strongest and most dynamic economies in the world, with pillar values above the world average for almost all pillars, except for the Competition pillar. These countries also show relatively less strength in Opportunity Perception and Startup Skills, for both of which they are close to the world average. Apart from Australia, the profiles of the mature Asia-Pacific countries are surprisingly uneven, suggesting systematic bottlenecks in Attitudes, balanced against notable strengths in Aspirations. As a general rule, the mature Asia-Pacific countries (with the exception of Australia) would appear to gain most by addressing this aspect of their entrepreneurial ecosystems.

We take a closer look at three different economies in the region (Fig. 4.9). Australia is a global leader that exhibits strength across virtually all GEI pillars. China is the world powerhouse in production, whose economic growth nevertheless has slowed down recently. Vietnam is an up-and-coming emerging economy with a large young population.

We see that Australia's entrepreneurial profile is quite round, which explains its high overall ranking. It also means that Australia is a strong all-around performer in terms of its entrepreneurial ecosystem. Australia's greatest strengths are found in Internationalization, Risk Capital, Opportunity Startup, Human Capital, Startup Skills, and Technology Absorption. There are no real weaknesses in Australia's entrepreneurship ecosystem, although Networking, Product Innovation, and High Growth Pillars do not exhibit quite the same strength as its best performing pillars. For Product Innovation, Australia in fact ranks behind China. This suggests that,

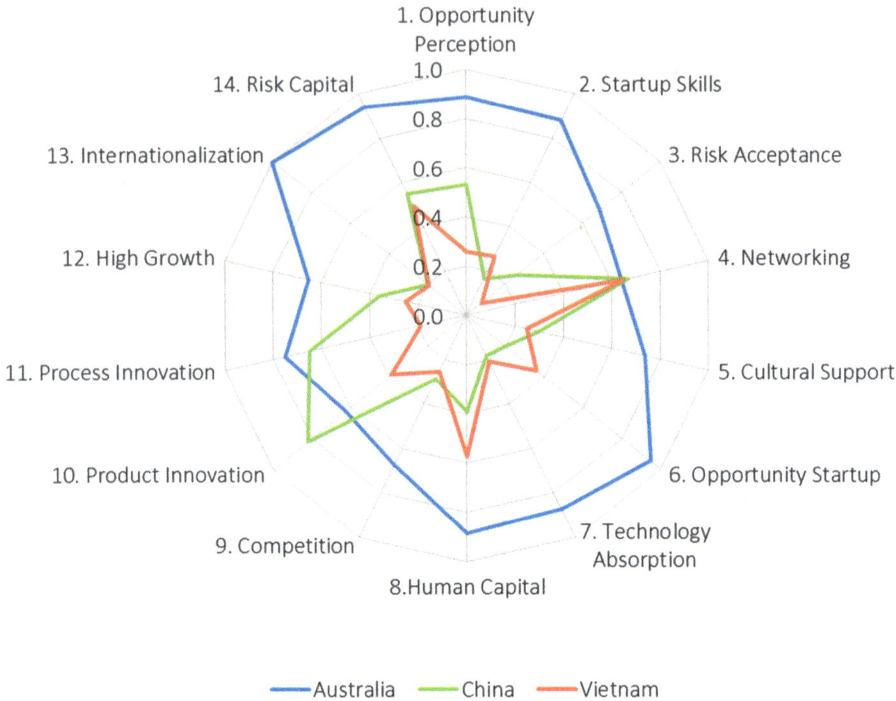

Fig. 4.9 Pillar-level comparison of Australia, China, and Vietnam

although Australia's overall innovation performance is strong, more of it could be channeled through the entrepreneurial sectors. Another relative weakness is found in Networking, suggesting that, even though Australia is a top performer globally, there are still areas where it can make further progress.

In contrast, China's profile of is very uneven. Its main strengths are in Aspirations—Product Innovation, Process Innovation, and Risk Capital. China also exhibits individual strengths within the other sub-indices, notably, Networking and Opportunity Perception. China's major bottlenecks appear to be in Internationalization, Startup Skills, and Opportunity Startup. Thus, there is an interesting contrast, in that China's high level of Opportunity Perception does not appear to be fully converted into Opportunity Startup activity. Because of China's large size and great internal diversity, with an industrialized east coast and rural west, general policy prescriptions are not feasible for this country. Clearly, China needs to adopt a regionalized approach to developing its national entrepreneurship ecosystem as a network of regional entrepreneurial ecosystems. China's highly uneven GEI profile suggests that it has the potential to achieve major progress by focusing its policy effort on bottleneck areas. The priority in China appears to be developing its institutional infrastructure for business.

Compared to Australia and China, Vietnam's entrepreneurial ecosystem profile is considerably less developed. There are, however, a number of bright spots.

In Networking, Vietnam ranks on par with Australia and China. In Human Capital, Vietnam outperforms China, and in Risk Capital, it is on a par with China. However, there are also notable weaknesses. Vietnam's score on Risk Acceptance is alarmingly low, and it ranks far behind China for Product and Process Innovation. As Vietnam seeks to strengthen its position as a low-end manufacturing hub, it also needs to consider investing in Innovation Strengths and Technology Absorption so as to move up the value chain.

4.4 Europe

Europe is also a region with notable internal divides. The entrepreneurially mature Europe consists of the "old" Western and Northern European countries (Table 4.5). These are some of the most developed and mature economies worldwide, which shows in the GEI rankings: Denmark is ranked as the fourth most entrepreneurial economy globally, and six of the top ten global performers are found in Northern and Western Europe. Moreover, 13 out of the top 20 entrepreneurial economies are from Western and Northern Europe, and all EU countries rank in the top 50 percent globally. These developed European economies exhibit traditional strengths in technology and innovation, and new European businesses can benefit from the EU's internal market and the high quality of its infrastructure and institutional set-up.

On the other hand, there is also a "developing Europe" that comprises the former centrally planned European economies. This region also includes Russia and Ukraine. Given its socialist history, developing Europe carries a legacy of an industry infrastructure biased toward heavy industries, a weak tradition of entrepreneurial activity, and, perhaps most importantly, a weak tradition of initiative and assumption of responsibility. While historically strong in human capital, developing Europe is held back by poor institutional conditions. Being inculcated primarily in industry structure and individual attitudes, the post-socialist legacy may prove surprisingly resilient and can perhaps ultimately be erased only through generational change (Fig. 4.10).

A closer look at the European countries offers further notable observations. The Nordic countries (Sweden, Denmark, Iceland, Finland, and Norway) all rank in the top 20 globally. France shows good strength, thanks to its high-quality infrastructure. Estonia performs strongly and ranks ahead of Luxembourg, Spain, Portugal, and Italy, among others. All three Baltic countries (Estonia, Lithuania, and Latvia) are closely ranked. Turkey (which we include in Europe in this analysis) performs strongly, splitting the Baltic countries. Italy's performance, on the other hand, is worryingly weak, as it ranks below Portugal, Spain, and Greece, a group of countries that have suffered badly in the wake of the global financial crisis that started in 2008. Indeed, Italy performs worse than many countries with socialist legacies, such as the Baltic countries, Slovenia, the Czech Republic, and even Romania, Bulgaria, and Hungary. This is an alarming situation, especially given that Italy's ranking appears to be on a downward trend. Italy's GEI score has collapsed from

Table 4.5 GEI ranking of the European countries

GEI rank	Country	ATT	ABT	ASP	GEI
4	Denmark	71.1	87.1	69.9	76.0
5	Sweden	77.3	79.9	70.4	75.9
7	Iceland	70.2	69.8	66.8	68.9
8	Switzerland	63.4	68.9	71.0	67.8
9	United Kingdom	70.9	73.3	58.8	67.7
10	France	58.3	73.4	67.4	66.4
12	Ireland	59.0	71.3	66.6	65.6
13	Netherlands	71.7	66.4	58.2	65.4
14	Germany	60.1	67.4	66.2	64.6
15	Austria	64.5	63.7	60.6	62.9
17	Belgium	53.4	62.4	70.4	62.1
18	Finland	72.1	52.5	60.7	61.8
20	Norway	69.9	68.3	45.1	61.1
22	Estonia	56.5	57.2	58.3	57.3
23	Luxembourg	44.0	65.7	62.0	57.2
25	Lithuania	47.9	58.2	58.2	54.8
26	Latvia	47.8	55.3	57.4	53.5
28	Turkey	49.7	46.2	62.1	52.7
31	Slovenia	47.6	49.8	53.9	50.4
32	Spain	54.5	52.6	43.4	50.2
33	Portugal	46.9	50.4	52.7	50.0
34	Poland	51.3	37.8	59.0	49.3
37	Slovakia	44.1	36.2	58.8	46.4
41	Hungary	43.4	45.3	46.7	45.1
42	Romania	38.2	40.8	55.9	44.9
44	Czech Republic	36.0	41.1	55.6	44.2
45	Greece	37.2	49.0	40.0	42.1
46	Bulgaria	41.8	34.7	48.5	41.6
48	Italy	35.7	37.3	50.2	41.1
49	Cyprus	32.4	51.3	39.4	41.0
51	Croatia	35.9	35.3	48.4	39.9
54	Montenegro	40.6	30.4	41.5	37.5
57	Macedonia	35.0	35.8	39.0	36.6
63	Ukraine	28.6	33.0	39.0	33.5
68	Russia	33.9	36.7	26.1	32.2
72	Moldova	24.9	35.9	33.1	31.3
74	Serbia	39.0	23.3	30.4	30.9
76	Albania	30.7	31.5	27.8	30.0
81	Georgia	25.7	34.9	25.5	28.7
82	Bosnia and Herzegovina	27.8	28.6	29.5	28.6
	Europe	48.5	51.0	51.9	50.4

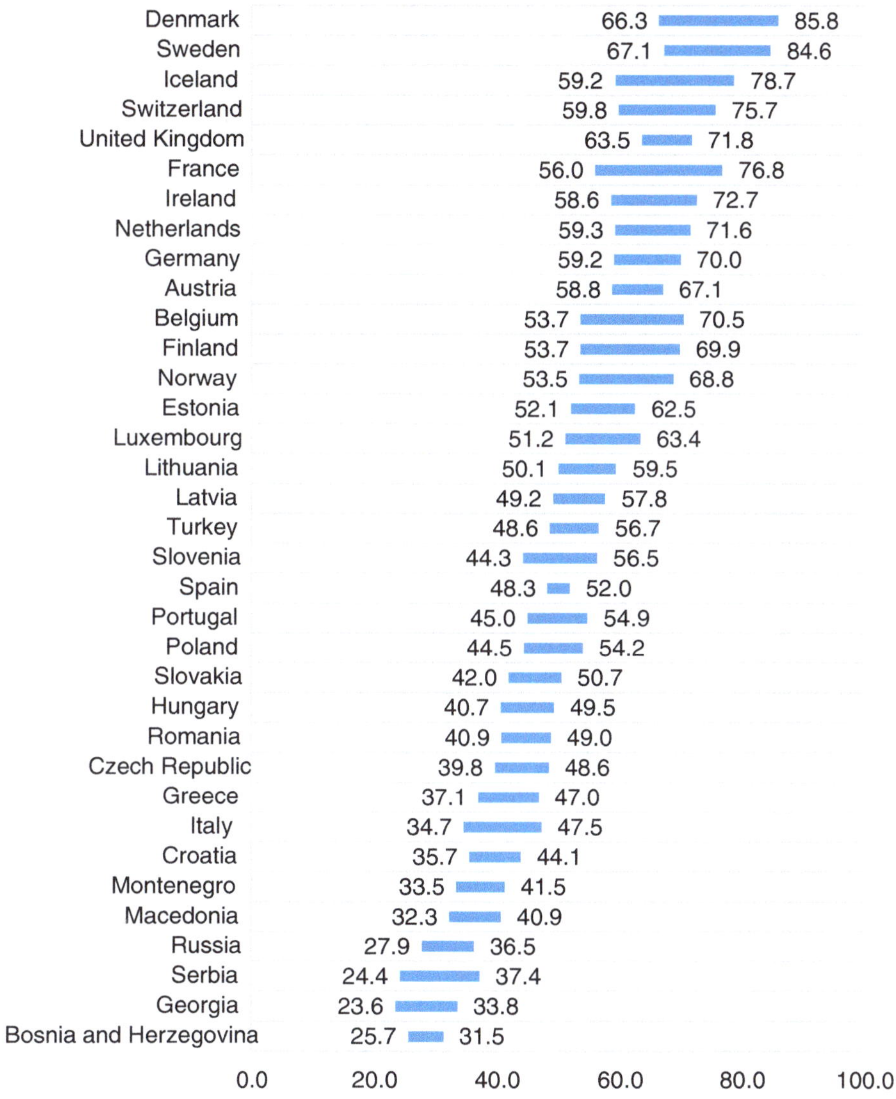

Fig. 4.10 Confidence intervals for the European countries (**Countries with estimated individual data are not shown, as confidence intervals for these countries cannot be calculated)

57.6 in 2008 to 41.1 in the current ranking. Thus, in 5 years, Italy's GEI score has dropped by over 15 points. The bottom performers in Europe are Ukraine, Russia, Moldova, Serbia, Albania, and Bosnia and Herzegovina.

In spite of Europe's heterogeneity, the combined pillar performance for this region is consistently above the world average, except for Opportunity Perception, where it is at the world average (Fig. 4.11). The Opportunity Perception mean is dragged down primarily by the former centrally planned economies in Europe. The

Fig. 4.11 Pillar-level comparison of Europe and the world

region's greatest strengths are found in Internationalization, Networking, Technology Absorption, Startup Skills, Process Innovation, and Risk Capital.

A closer look at three European entrepreneurial ecosystems reveals notable heterogeneity among European countries. The region's leading entrepreneurial economy, Denmark, exhibits a strong all-around entrepreneurial profile. In contrast, Greece and Russia have much catching up to do, with their considerably more uneven profiles (Fig. 4.12).

Denmark has a strong entrepreneurial economy, and its GEI rankings are consistently at or close to the top in the world. This shows in its GEI profile, which is very round, suggesting a strong all-around performance. Denmark's greatest strengths are found in the Abilities pillars (Opportunity Startup, Technology Absorption, Human Capital, and Competition), where its scores are almost perfect. Denmark also exhibits strength in Product Innovation and Risk Capital. Somewhat surprisingly, Internationalization is Denmark's most important bottleneck, together with Startup Skills. In addition, the scores for High Growth and Risk Acceptance also could be improved.

In contrast, Greece appears to exhibit both outstanding strengths and notable bottlenecks. Greece's strongest pillar is Startup Skills, but this may be partly due to the large grey economy in the country, and perhaps also due to the small business orientation of the Greek economy, which features few high-growth businesses.

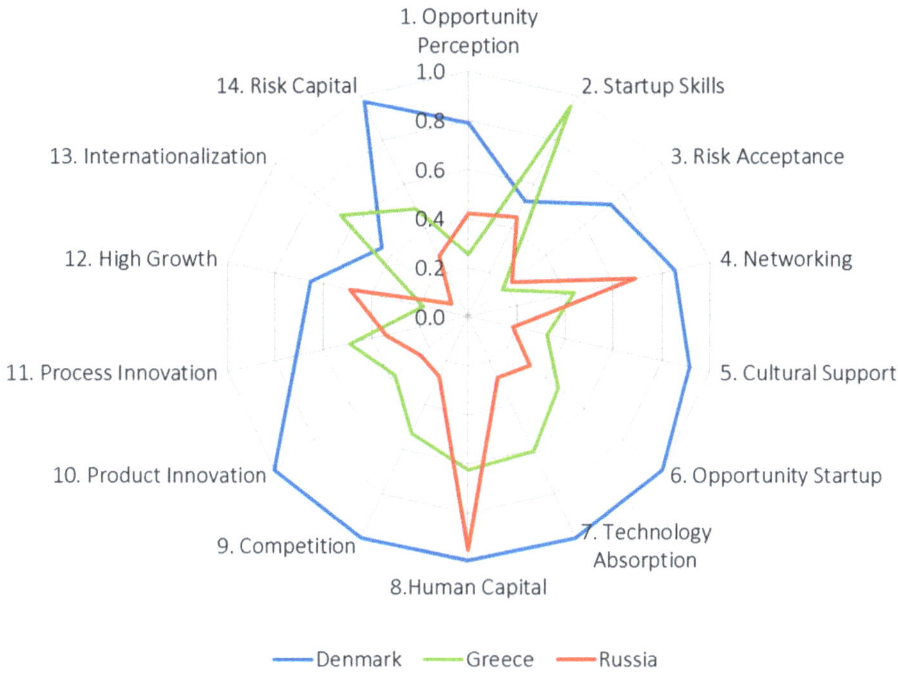

Fig. 4.12 Pillar-level comparison of Denmark, Greece, and Russia

Greece also exhibits reasonable strength in Internationalization, Human Capital, and Technology Absorption. On the other hand, Greece exhibits major bottlenecks in Risk Acceptance, High Growth, Cultural Support, and Opportunity Perception. It may well be that this uneven profile has been influenced by the deep recession that Greece entered in 2008. The recent turmoil in Greece has further aggravated the situation, and there is much catching up to do. Perhaps the biggest area to address is Greece's notorious bureaucracy, which is a real hindrance to its entrepreneurial potential. This is reflected in its low scores in High Growth and in Risk Acceptance. While much has been done to address this constraint and move economic activity from the grey economy to the formal economy, Greece has much work to do in harnessing its entrepreneurial potential for economic growth. As it faces these challenges, Greece might draw inspiration from Iceland and Ireland, both of which were hard hit by the economic downturn, but have emerged from the recession and reentered a growth path.

Russia's entrepreneurship profile exhibits similar unevenness. In spite of its extensive natural resources, the Russian entrepreneurial ecosystem is the fifth weakest in Europe. This suggests that, instead of being a source of strength, the resource abundance of the Russian economy can actually be a source of weakness, as it has led Russia to become increasingly dependent on the spot market price of oil for its economic wealth. Helped by the favorable development of oil prices until recently, this abundance has also allowed Russian politicians to fail to introduce the political and economic reforms needed to facilitate innovation and the diversification of the Russian industrial base. In fact, rather than diversifying, the Russian industrial base has become even more reliant on energy and raw materials. These developments have resulted in an entrepreneurial profile that is highly uneven and lags behind most post-socialist countries. The outstanding Russian strength is Human Capital, followed by much weaker Networking (perhaps consistent with the Russian tradition of *blat* and High Growth. These relative strengths are offset by bottlenecks in Internationalization, Cultural Support, Product Innovation, Competition, Risk Acceptance, and Process Innovation. Laden with post-socialist baggage, the Russian entrepreneurial ecosystem continues to exhibit many deficiencies, and the Russian economy's lack of diversification and dependence on energy and raw materials do not help with the prevailing governance structure. It appears that, to escape this dilemma, Russia needs to considerably strengthen its rule of law and economic and political institutions.

4.5 North America

In our analysis, North America includes the NAFTA countries: the US, Canada, and Mexico. Of these, the US and Canada are global leaders, ranking 1st and 2nd in the global GEI ranking (Table 4.6). In contrast, Mexico only ranks 87th· despite some positive progress in recent years. Whereas the profiles of the US and Canada show approximately equal strength for all sub-indices, Mexico appears to be strong in Attitudes, but its entrepreneurial performance is held back by weaknesses in Abilities and Aspirations (Fig. 4.13).

Dominated by the US economy, the North American region exhibits traditional strength in entrepreneurship. This is illustrated by Fig. 4.14, which shows the GEI profile of the North American region compared against the world average. North America stands out as the strongest entrepreneurial ecosystem in the GEI analysis, with all pillars clearly above the world average. Particular strength is exhibited in Opportunity Perception, but the region performs strongly across all pillars. Overall, the profile of this region is relatively round, dominated by the US and Canada.

In Fig. 4.15 we compare all three countries in this region. The US is the leading entrepreneurial ecosystem in North America, and it also ranks first globally. A traditional hotspot for entrepreneurship, the US boasts strengths in all areas, the only possible exception being Networking. This could signal the highly individualistic

Table 4.6 GEI ranking of the North American countries

GEI rank	Country	ATT	ABT	ASP	GEI
1	United States	84.4	84.8	89.5	86.2
2	Canada	78.1	81.3	79.0	79.5
87	Mexico	40.8	20.8	21.3	27.6
	North America average	67.8	62.3	63.3	64.4

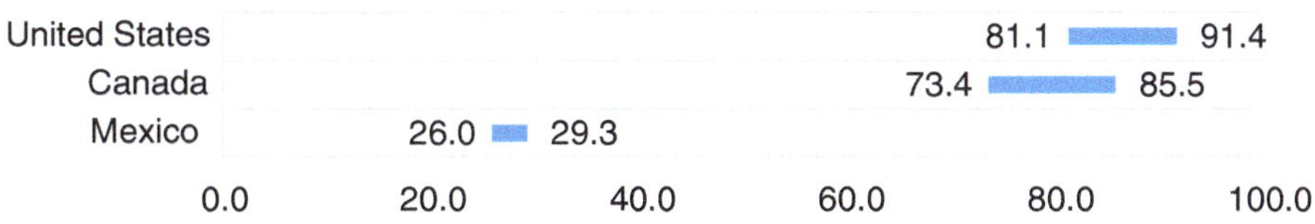

Fig. 4.13 Confidence intervals for the North American countries

Fig. 4.14 Pillar-level comparison of North America and the world

US culture and suggests that Networking—which is an important requirement in the knowledge economy—is be an area where concentrated policy efforts could bring about the greatest returns.

Canada's entrepreneurial profile is quite similar to that of the US, which is reflected in the global ranking of the Canadian entrepreneurial ecosystem (2nd). Relative to the US, Canada exhibits some softness in Startup Skills, Product and Process Innovation, High Growth, and Competition. Thus it appears that Canada should invest further in entrepreneurship education and training, and in Innovation. One strength of the Canadian economy is that it is close to a large market and can tap into the strengths of the US entrepreneurial ecosystem.

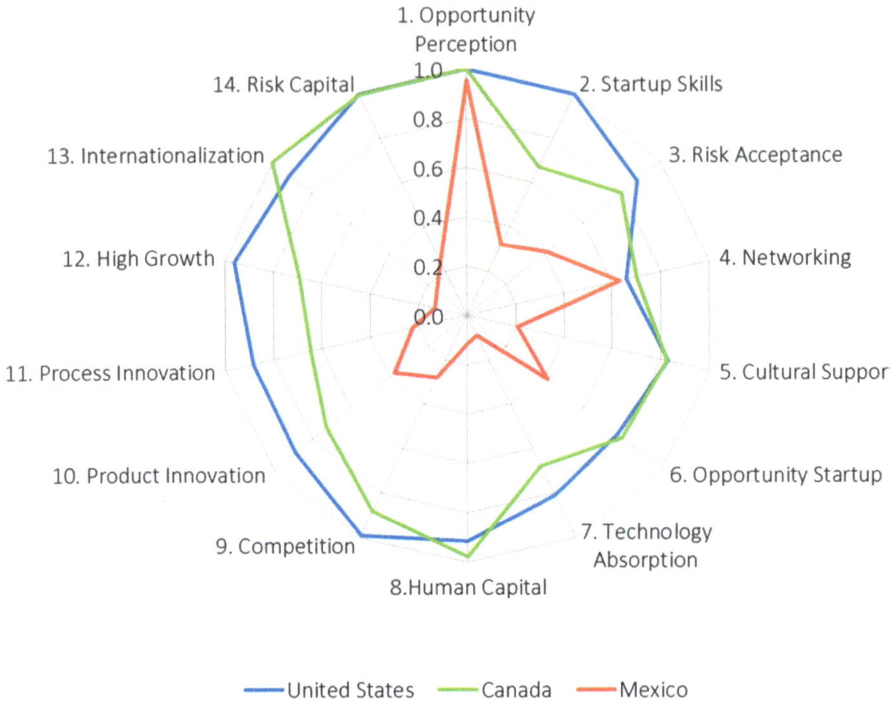

Fig. 4.15 Pillar-level comparison of the United States, Canada, and Mexico

Mexico's entrepreneurial ecosystem is considerably less developed than that of the US and Canada. Although it exhibits strength in Opportunity Perception and to some degree in Networking, Opportunity Startup, and Product Innovation, the Mexican entrepreneurial ecosystem suffers from clear bottlenecks in Technology Absorption, Internationalization, Human Capital, High Growth, and Cultural Support. Thus, whereas Mexico's strength is primarily in Attitudes, its bottlenecks are mostly concentrated in Aspirations; however, notable bottlenecks are also found in Attitudes and Abilities. It seems that Mexico would need a broad-based, coordinated policy program to address its bottlenecks without undermining its strengths.

4.6 South and Central America and Caribbean

In this analysis, the South and Central America and Caribbean region includes all Latin American economies except Mexico (Table 4.7). Although considerably less developed than North America and developed Europe and Asia, this region offers considerable potential for entrepreneurial activity, thanks to its overall growing economy, improving governance, and young population. Many Latin American economies have recorded positive developments in recent years, although progress

Table 4.7 GEI ranking of the South and Central American and Caribbean countries

GEI rank	Country	ATT	ABT	ASP	GEI
16	Chile	74.9	47.9	63.4	62.1
35	Puerto Rico	50.6	56.6	37.1	48.1
43	Colombia	45.3	39.8	49.3	44.8
47	Uruguay	50.3	40.8	32.9	41.3
53	Barbados	48.2	38.9	28.3	38.5
58	Costa Rica	46.9	32.8	28.8	36.2
61	Argentina	43.6	31.1	29.7	34.8
67	Panama	41.2	34.7	21.5	32.4
69	Bolivia	37.3	27.7	31.5	32.1
70	Peru	44.9	27.7	23.5	32.0
71	Dominican Republic	41.0	26.4	27.7	31.7
77	Belize	27.0	39.2	23.0	29.8
83	Trinidad & Tobago	29.9	32.2	22.6	28.2
88	Ecuador	35.7	25.8	20.7	27.4
90	Jamaica	35.2	28.4	18.3	27.3
92	Brazil	41.9	23.7	12.6	26.1
93	Paraguay	32.0	25.7	20.1	26.0
96	El Salvador	28.0	29.4	19.4	25.6
100	Venezuela	39.2	17.0	16.0	24.1
105	Honduras	22.4	25.9	17.3	21.9
107	Guatemala	23.5	21.6	18.3	21.1
108	Guyana	18.2	27.0	14.3	19.8
110	Nicaragua	21.0	23.0	14.3	19.4
111	Suriname	24.3	21.4	12.3	19.3
	South and Central America/Caribbean average	37.6	31.0	25.1	31.2

has been far from uniform. While some countries have instituted strong and open governance systems (e.g., Chile and Uruguay), the continent overall continues to suffer from incompetent governance that holds back its entrepreneurial potential (Fig. 4.16).

In this region, the top performer is Chile, which is also the only country in the region that ranks in the top 20 in the global GEI ranking (16th). Puerto Rico and Colombia are behind Chile and close to one another, followed by Uruguay. After Uruguay, there is a cluster of several countries with similar GEI scores: Barbados, Costa Rica, and Argentina. It is notable that Brazil only ranks 16th among the 23 countries in this group, although this represents an improvement over the previous year, when it ranked 19th. Note that the GEI ranking does not cover Cuba and Haiti, both of which would likely rank close to the bottom.

Collectively, the relative strengths in this group are found in Attitudes and Abilities, whereas the region's performance in Aspirations is relatively weak. The region thus faces a challenge in improving Aspirations and in instilling a more inno-

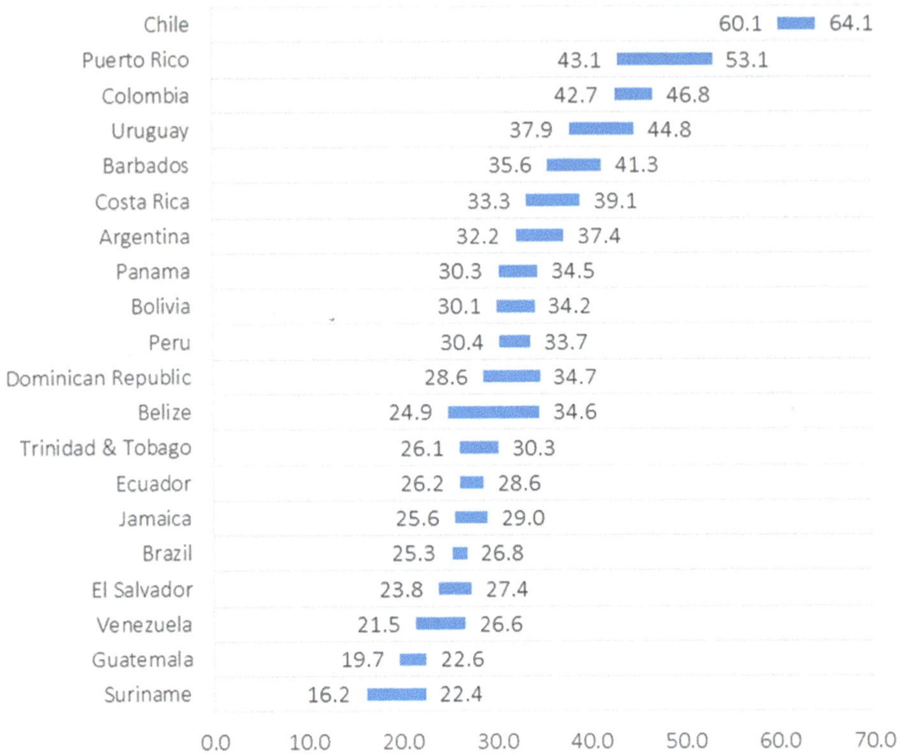

Fig. 4.16 Confidence intervals for South and Central American and Caribbean countries (**Countries with estimated individual data are not shown, as confidence intervals for these countries cannot be calculated)

vative, growth-oriented, and international outlook among its population of entrepreneurs. This challenge appears particularly acute in Brazil, which ranks near the bottom of the region in this regard. Like most countries in this region, Brazil should look to Chile and Colombia for inspiration on how to improve its entrepreneurial aspirations.

As a group, the GEI profile of the South and Central American and Caribbean region is quite uneven (Fig. 4.17). The region exhibits strengths that beat the world average in Opportunity Perception and Startup Skills, but it is at or lags behind the world average in other pillars, notably in Process Innovation, Risk Capital, and Technology Absorption. In spite of these challenges, this region offers great potential for entrepreneurship, conditioned by its ability to strengthen its economic institutions and governance systems.

We look at three countries in this region: Chile, Argentina, and Belize (Fig. 4.18). Chile boasts the strongest entrepreneurial ecosystem in this region, thanks perhaps to its strong, market-embracing governance systems. Globally, Chile has improved from 19th to 16th in the 2016 GEI ranking, despite its relatively low (globally speaking) GDP per capita, which is clearly the smallest among the top 20 entrepre-

Fig. 4.17 Pillar-level comparison of South and Central American and Caribbean and the world

neurial economies in the GEI ranking. In fact, the second lowest GDP per capita in the top 20 is exhibited by France, whose GDP per capita is almost double that of Chile. This is a remarkable achievement, given that the quality of institutions tends to be strongly correlated with economic wealth, and the quality of institutions is also given considerable weight in the Index. Thus, Chile "punches above its weight" in entrepreneurship—an outcome that we attribute to the country's sound governance systems. The most important strengths of the Chilean system are Opportunity Perception, Product Innovation, and Startup Skills, with the most important bottlenecks found in Process Innovation, Competition, and Technology Absorption. Chile exhibits the greatest overall strength in Attitudes, followed by Aspirations and Abilities.

Argentina is among the largest economies in this region, where it ranks 7th; it ranks 61st in the overall GEI ranking. Argentina exhibits considerably weaker governance systems, and economic and political institutions, than Chile. These handicaps prevent Argentina from taking full advantage of its large consumer market, which is reflected in the country's entrepreneurial profile. Although the country exhibits strengths in Startup Skills and Opportunity Perception, it also exhibits important weaknesses in Risk Acceptance, Internationalization, Cultural Support,

Fig. 4.18 Pillar-level comparison of Chile, Argentina, and Belize

and Opportunity Startup. Argentina's spiky profile suggests that there are several bottlenecks it should make it a priority to address.

Belize is a good example of the small South/Central American countries. Bordered by Mexico and Guatemala, It ranks 12th in the region for its entrepreneurial ecosystem, after the Dominican Republic but ahead of Trinidad & Tobago. In contrast with Argentina, Belize shows strength in Competition and Opportunity Startup, with its most important weaknesses in Opportunity Perception and Risk Capital. Belize ranks 77th in the overall global GEI ranking. The spiky profile of its entrepreneurial ecosystem suggests that Belize, like Argentina, could achieve considerable progress in entrepreneurship by addressing its systemic bottlenecks.

Chapter 5
Enhancing Entrepreneurial Ecosystems: A GEI Approach to Entrepreneurship Policy

5.1 Entrepreneurial Ecosystems: Challenge to Traditional Policymaking

Facilitating entrepreneurship is high on many government policy agendas. Policies that support entrepreneurship have become increasingly sophisticated over time, as governments have moved from facilitating the creation of new firms toward supporting high-growth businesses. Many governments currently talk about support ecosystems that cover the entire life cycle of a new venture, from inception to early survival and growth to international expansion. Many governments have adopted a focus on high-growth firms, having learned that only a small fraction of all new firms end up creating the bulk of new jobs.

Unfortunately, although high-growth entrepreneurship and entrepreneurial ecosystems are high on many policy agendas, there is fairly little understanding of how policy can foster them most effectively. Most entrepreneurship policy playbooks remain stuck with old world policy approaches, which focus on identifying and fixing "market failures" and "structural failures." Such approaches, while effective in addressing well-specified market and structural failures, are hopelessly inadequate to deal with the complexities of entrepreneurial ecosystems.

A classic example of a market failure is the failure of businesses to invest in R&D. Because R&D is a risky and uncertain activity, many firms are tempted to wait, to let others to take the risk, and then quickly copy successful projects. But if everyone thought this way, no one would invest in R&D, and innovative activities would stagnate. Therefore, governments address this market failure by providing subsidies for R&D—in effect, participating in the downside risk while allowing firms to keep the upside returns.

In contrast to subsidizing specific activities, a structural failure policy would seek to build support services and structures that support new firm creation and growth. Examples of structural failure policies include, for example, the creation of science parks and business incubators to shelter and support startup ventures.

Z. Acs et al., *Global Entrepreneurship and Development Index 2016*,
SpringerBriefs in Economics, DOI 10.1007/978-3-319-63844-7_5

Both of these approaches fail to address the complexities of entrepreneurial ecosystems, which are too complex to allow easy identification of specific clean-cut market failures, such as insufficient investment in R&D. The "product" entrepreneurial ecosystems produce is innovative and high-growth new ventures. Creating high-growth new ventures is a far more complex undertaking than starting an R&D project. If we do not see a sufficient number of high-growth new ventures, where exactly is the market failure supposed to reside? The standard approach by governments, which is consistent with market failure thinking, is that there perhaps is not sufficient support funding available to start new, high-growth firms. However, as much as governments have provided subsidies to support new firm creation, the results have not been very encouraging.

As regards structural failure policies, how many more science parks can be built? After significant investment in building science parks and similar facilities, we have learned that these parks alone are not very effective in facilitating high-growth businesses. Again, to be effective, an entrepreneurial ecosystem policy needs to go beyond simply building walls and toward facilitating entire ecosystems.

Another major problem with both market failure and structural failure approaches is that they are top-down, where the policymaker analyzes, designs, and implements entrepreneurship policy. Top-down, however, is not a feasible approach in entrepreneurial ecosystems that consist of multiple independent stakeholders. In such situations, a policymaker cannot simply command and control, as you have no formal authority over ecosystem stakeholders. Instead, policymakers need to engage the various stakeholders and co-opt them as active participants and contributors to the policy intervention. In the following, we highlight distinctive characteristics of entrepreneurial ecosystems and elaborate related policy challenges. We then present the GEDI Stakeholder Approach to entrepreneurial ecosystem policy.

5.2 Entrepreneurial Ecosystems: Definitions and Policy Challenges

Entrepreneurial ecosystems are fundamentally interaction systems consisting of multiple, co-specialized, yet hierarchically independent stakeholders, many of which may not even know one another. Here, co-specialization means that different stakeholders play different roles—venture capitalists, research institutions, different supporting institutions, new ventures, established businesses, and so on. They offer complementary skills and services, and normally depend on others to accomplish their goals, which implies that team play is needed.

In the above, hierarchical independence means that there are no formal lines of command, unlike, say, within government agencies or industrial corporations. Everyone makes their own independent decisions and optimizes their own performance. Combined with co-specialization, this creates a mutual dependency dilemma: to accomplish your goals you must depend on others, yet you cannot tell others what to do. Cooperation is therefore required. This limits the usability of

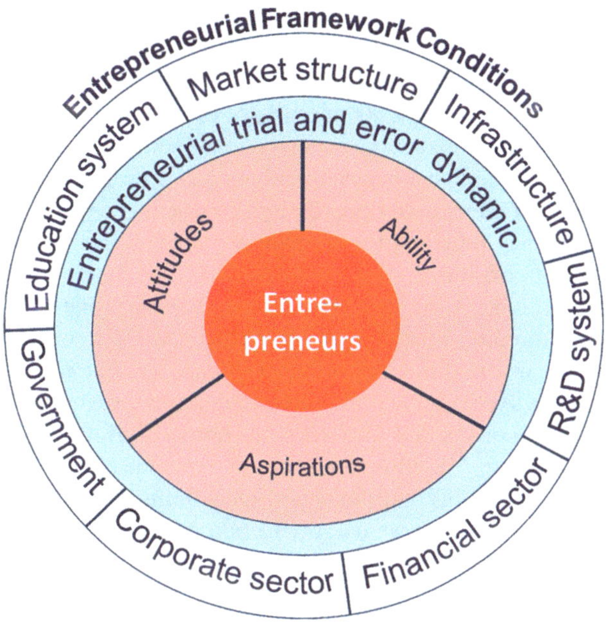

Fig. 5.1 GEI model of entrepreneurial ecosystems

traditional top-down policies, which are usually implemented through formal chains of command (e.g., a government department designing a policy, which is then implemented by a government agency overseen by the department).

Also of relevance is the notion of interaction systems, which means that the stakeholders of entrepreneurial ecosystems "co-produce" their outputs, such as innovative high-growth new ventures. These outputs are co-produced through a myriad of usually uncoordinated interactions between hierarchically independent yet interdependent stakeholders. This combination of independence and interdependence makes coordination challenging.

The structure of the entrepreneurial ecosystem is illustrated in Fig. 5.1. Nascent and new entrepreneurs are at the heart of the system. Nascent entrepreneurs are individuals in the process of launching a new venture. These entrepreneurs represent a sub-set of the adult population in a given country. The attitudes that prevail within the wider population influence who chooses to become an entrepreneur. The nascent and new entrepreneurs are characterized by varying degrees of ability and entrepreneurial aspirations.

In the GEI model, it is the entrepreneurs who drive the entrepreneurial trial-and-error dynamic. This means that entrepreneurs start new businesses to pursue opportunities that they themselves perceive. An entrepreneurial opportunity is simply a chance to make money through a new venture, such as producing and selling goods and services for profit. However, entrepreneurs can never tell in advance whether a given opportunity is real or not: the only way to validate an opportunity is to pursue it. In other words, entrepreneurs need to take risks: they need to access and mobilize resources (human, financial, physical, technological) before they can verify whether or not a profit can be made. This means, then, that not all entrepreneurial efforts will be successful, as some opportunities turn out to be mere mirages. In such cases, the budding entrepreneur will realize sooner or later that they are never going to make a profit, or that they could make more money doing something else. In such cases, the entrepreneur will abandon the current pursuit and do something else instead.

If, however, an entrepreneurial opportunity turns out to be real, the entrepreneurs will make more money pursuing that opportunity than doing something else, and they will continue to exploit it. The net outcome of this entrepreneurial trial-and-error dynamic, therefore, is the allocation of resources to productive uses. In other words, a healthy entrepreneurial dynamic within a given economy will drive total factor productivity, or the difference between inputs and outputs. The greater the total factor productivity, the greater the economy's capacity to create new wealth.

Entrepreneurs do not operate in a vacuum, however. Both the entrepreneurial choices individuals make (i.e., those who choose to pursue entrepreneurial opportunities and those who do not) and the wealth-generating potential of the resulting ventures are regulated by what we call the Entrepreneurial Framework Conditions that prevail in the country. There are two issues of importance here. First, there is the question of who chooses to become an entrepreneur and who chooses not to. This matters because individuals with higher human capital (i.e., better education, stronger abilities) are more likely to create innovative, high-growth ventures than individuals with low human capital. If high-potential individuals choose not to pursue such opportunities, the entrepreneurial dynamic will suffer. Second, there is the question of how likely the new venture is to fulfill its potential. A new venture created in a resource-poor environment (say, a poorly developed country) is less likely to fulfill its growth potential than if it were created in an entrepreneurial hotspot (say, London's Silicon Roundabout).

Entrepreneurial framework conditions matter because they regulate, first, who chooses to become an entrepreneur and, second, to what extent the resulting new ventures are able to fulfill their growth potential. The first aspect—entrepreneurial choice—is regulated mostly by "soft" framework conditions, such as social norms and cultural preferences. If well-educated individuals perceive entrepreneurship to be a valued and glamorous career choice, they are more likely to choose it over alternative career paths. This aspect is captured in the GEI entrepreneurial ecosystem model by Attitudes. The entrepreneurial choice is also regulated by "hard" factors, such as opportunity costs and the size of perceived opportunities. These aspects are regulated by all the framework conditions combined.

The degree to which new ventures are able to fulfill their potential is regulated by a range of entrepreneurial framework conditions, such as the market structure, physical infrastructure, R&D system, financial sector, corporate sector, government, and the education system. These framework conditions are listed in the outer circle of the GEI entrepreneurial ecosystem model. The government provides support, and it also creates flexible regulations and enforces the rule of law. The market structure defines the level of competition and the ease of market entry. The education system facilitates the creation of human capital, and also shapes attitudes toward entrepreneurship and builds entrepreneurial skills. The physical infrastructure impacts ease of trading. The R&D system provides technology inputs and feeds innovation. The financial sector provides financing—both equity and debt funding. The corporate sector provides important demand for new ventures, and an important exit mechanism.

The GEI model illustrates the complexity of entrepreneurial ecosystems and helps explain why traditional modes of policymaking often prove inadequate in addressing them. In a complex system such as the one illustrated in Fig. 5.1, it can be quite difficult to identify clear-cut market or structural failures. Rather, all elements of the ecosystem interact, often in surprising and difficult to predict ways, to influence individual-level entrepreneurial choices and the outcomes of those choices. The ecosystem service is created through the interactions of the different elements of the entrepreneurial ecosystem—that is, innovative, high-growth new ventures.

5.3 Using the GEI to Facilitate Entrepreneurial Ecosystems

The distinctive methodological features of the GEI are designed to capture the distinctive characteristics of entrepreneurial ecosystems, and thus facilitate effective policymaking for these ecosystems. It captures the entrepreneurial ecosystem dynamic by contextualizing individual-level data with data that describe a country's entrepreneurship framework conditions. It uses 14 context-weighted measures of entrepreneurial Attitudes, Abilities, and Aspirations, which are organized into three sub-indices. Importantly, it uses a Penalty of Bottleneck algorithm to both simulate co-production of system outputs through stakeholder interactions and facilitate the identification of bottleneck factors that hold back ecosystem performance. See Chap. 6 for a detailed description of the GEI method.

As explained in Chap. 6, each pillar of the GEI is measured as a composite of individual-level data and data that describe relevant framework conditions for entrepreneurship. For example, Startup Skills captures whether adult individuals think they have the necessary skills to start a new venture, weighted by a measure of the degree of tertiary education in the country. This framework variable is used because the higher a country's level of education the higher the quality of its entrepreneurial ventures tends to be. As another example, Networking is a combination of how many individuals in the adult population personally know people who have started new businesses, weighted by the prevalence of Internet use in the country. This measure is used because the Internet tends to amplify opportunities for networking. Thus, the GEI approach captures individual-level attitudes, abilities, and aspirations; each individual variable is then weighted by a relevant framework condition that regulates a given individual-level variable's potential to contribute to a high-quality entrepreneurial dynamic. In other words, this approach captures the notion that entrepreneurial ecosystems are brought to life by individuals, but the ultimate impact of individual-level action is regulated by entrepreneurial framework conditions.

The GEI methodology captures two other important aspects that define entrepreneurial ecosystems. First, it recognizes that the different pillars need to work together to create a high-quality ecosystem dynamic. Traditional indexes fail to capture this aspect. In traditional indexing methods, the different components (pillars) are allowed to substitute for one another. In other words, a traditional index would allow, say, Risk Capital to compensate for the Quality of Human Resources. This notion of substitutability is similar to replacing eggs with flour when baking a cake. Everyone knows that you need both eggs and flour to bake a good cake, and the GEI methodology similarly requires that a high-quality entrepreneurial dynamic needs both Risk Capital and High-Quality Human Resources, in addition to the system's 12 other pillars. If one or more pillars perform poorly, it is likely to hold back the performance of the entire system. Although one in reality can compensate to some degree for, say, Human Resources with Risk Capital, the entrepreneurial ecosystem is likely to ground to a halt if either element is completely absent.

The notion of bottlenecks derives directly from the notion that ecosystem elements interact to co-produce ecosystem performance. Because one cannot fully substitute individual pillars for others, poorly performing pillars can create bottlenecks that prevent the ecosystem from fully leveraging its strengths. To simulate this effect, the GEI methodology applies the Penalty for Bottleneck algorithm, which is explained in Chap. 6. This algorithm systematically penalizes ecosystem pillars according to its poorly performing pillars. By highlighting potential constraining factors in the entrepreneurial ecosystem, the PFB algorithm guides policy attention to the aspects of the ecosystem that may benefit most from coordinated policy action.

These methodological innovations of the GEI provide important insights into the workings of entrepreneurial ecosystems. Essential to the bottlenecks notion is that some factors may unduly constrain system performance beyond their objective importance. With the PFB methodology, it is possible to identify both where bottlenecks might lurk in any given system and how much the system performance will suffer as a result. These are strengths that no other index approach can offer and that make the GEI approach ideally suited to analyzing entrepreneurial ecosystems.

5.4 GEI Approach for Entrepreneurial Ecosystem Policy Analysis

To illustrate the GEI PFB method, consider a comparison between the US, Japan, and India, as shown in Fig. 5.2. The figure shows the entrepreneurial ecosystem profiles of the three countries, as measured by the GEI approach.

Figure 5.2 shows that the GEI profile of the US entrepreneurial ecosystem is round, with each pillar showing a strong performance. This is the hallmark of a well-balanced entrepreneurial ecosystem. The absence of major gaps in the US GEI profile means that no major bottlenecks are holding back the performance of the US

Fig. 5.2 Entrepreneurial ecosystem profiles of the US, Japan, and India

entrepreneurial ecosystem. There is relative softness in the US ecosystem in terms of Networking and Internationalization, which indicates that the US is not as strong in these areas. The relative softness in Internationalization is understandable, as the large size of the US domestic market makes it possible for entrepreneurs to grow a business without having to export their products or services.

Japan's ecosystem profile is considerably more uneven than that of the US, which suggests that the Japanese entrepreneurial ecosystem suffers from real bottlenecks that hold back its performance. The biggest bottlenecks are in Startup Skills, Opportunity Perception, Internationalization, and Competition. If Japan is seeking to improve its entrepreneurial performance, it should prioritize these areas. Addressing Startup Skills is relatively straightforward, as it can be addressed with education policies. These policies would likely also strengthen Opportunity Perception, although this pillar also depends on the country's general economic performance. Like the US, Japan's large domestic market probably moderates its Internationalization aspirations. Addressing the Competition pillar likely requires altogether different policies.

The profile of India's entrepreneurial ecosystem is considerably less developed and more uneven than those of the US and Japan. This pattern is typical of developing economies. The biggest bottlenecks for the India's ecosystem are observed in Opportunity Startup, Internationalization, High Growth, Product Innovation, and

Startup Skills. The low level of Opportunity Startups contrasts interestingly with a relatively healthy level of Opportunity Perception, which is actually at a higher level in India than in Japan. This suggests that India's infamous red tape perhaps inhibits the conversion of perceived opportunities into opportunity-driven businesses. The low level of Startup Skills no doubt contributes to this imbalance. As a developing economy, India could make considerable progress simply by addressing its basic framework conditions for entrepreneurial and economic activity, such as the rule of law (i.e., equality, objectivity, and predictability in the application of laws, rules, and regulations), equal access to markets, and human capital. It is likely that all developing economies need to address such basic conditions, but the GEI analysis helps highlight specific priority areas for India.

The above examples show how the GEI method could be harnessed for use in the analysis and design of entrepreneurial ecosystem policies in different economic contexts. Merely examining the ecosystem profiles of different countries provides interesting clues about country-specific features and the determinants of the quality of a country's entrepreneurial ecosystem. This is important, because it helps policymakers focus on areas that appear to be constraining a country's entrepreneurial performance. A considerably more detailed analysis can be made by focusing on individual pillar components (only pillar-level analysis was shown here) and choosing benchmarks that are at a similar level of economic development. For example, it probably does not make sense to compare India to the US because the two economies are so different. Better insights could perhaps be gained by comparing India to, say, China, Pakistan, or even a more aspirational benchmark such as Malaysia.

This analysis can be taken much further. For example, because the GEI methodology allows the ecosystem pillars to interact, it is possible to conduct sensitivity analyses and simulate different policy scenarios. For example, in a recent policy analysis for the Scottish Enterprise, we analyzed where additional policy efforts should be focused in Scotland and other UK Home Nations (i.e., England, Northern Ireland, and Wales) in order to achieve a 10% increase in the overall GEI score. This analysis is presented in Table 5.1, which shows how the additional policy efforts should be allocated across the ecosystem pillars, assuming equal cost to increase pillar performance. The GEI methodology for Scotland, for example, suggests that 13% of the additional policy effort should be allocated to Opportunity Perception, 12% to Risk Capital, 11% each to Startup Skills, Networking, and Process Innovation, and so on.

These figures were calculated by focusing policy efforts on the most pressing bottleneck until it was alleviated, then moving to the next most pressing bottleneck, and so on. While this example obviously includes a number of simplifying assumptions (notably, equal cost to address each pillar; an equally applied bottleneck penalty for all pillars; pillars' equal ability to be changed by policy action), it nevertheless demonstrates the GEI methodology's ability to assess different policy scenarios. Although the scenarios should not be taken as prescriptive, the exercise nevertheless highlights priority areas that could be explored further. Another important benefit is that even this simplifying analysis suggests that there may be important differences among the UK Home Nations in terms of policy priorities in facilitating the UK's entrepreneurial ecosystem.

Table 5.1 Ecosystem optimization analysis for UK Home Nations

	Scotland	Wales	N. Ireland	England	UK
Opportunity perception	13%	21%	24%	8%	9%
Startup skills	11%	11%	13%	8%	9%
NonFear of failure	4%	3%	6%	5%	5%
Networking	11%	11%	9%	9%	9%
Cultural support	3%	0%	0%	6%	6%
Opportunity startup	4%	3%	1%	5%	5%
Tech sector	0%	6%	0%	0%	0%
Quality of human resources	4%	3%	5%	4%	4%
Competition	0%	0%	0%	3%	3%
Product innovation	9%	9%	6%	10%	10%
Process innovation	11%	11%	13%	9%	9%
High growth	9%	6%	7%	11%	10%
Internationalization	7%	6%	4%	10%	10%
Risk capital	12%	11%	12%	13%	11%
	100%	100%	100%	100%	100%

5.5 Using the GEI Method for Entrepreneurial Ecosystem Policy Implementation

While the GEI provides the most innovative and powerful platform for entrepreneurial ecosystem policy analysis and design, important challenges remain. As noted above, a number of simplifying assumptions are needed to apply a PFB algorithm in constructing the Index. Such assumptions should be kept in mind when using the GEI approach to simulate the kind of policy scenarios illustrated in Table 5.1. As such, the choice of the ecosystem pillars themselves could be debated. For example, different framework measures might be required when developing a regional version of the GEI, as was done when a version was designed for the 125 EU regions. Importantly, the scenarios in Table 5.1 imply that there may not be one optimal ecosystem configuration for each country and each level of economic development. In fact, it is highly likely that there may be several efficient configurations for different countries at the same level of economic development, and for those at different levels of economic development. As noted earlier, entrepreneurial ecosystems are complex and there is still a great deal to learn about how they really work.

One important limitation of the GEI methodology is that it only uses hard data. Entrepreneurial ecosystems are inherently complex, and this complexity extends beyond the quantification of individual ecosystem pillars. The GEI profile indicates which elements of the entrepreneurial ecosystem are in place and in what quantity; however, much like using the same ingredients can produce very different outcomes when baking a cake, depending on how the ingredients are mixed, the GEI tells us little about how the elements should be mixed to produce the best possible outcome for any given country. These soft aspects of entrepreneurial ecosystems are hard to capture using only hard data. Therefore, to facilitate entrepreneurship policy design, it is important to blend hard and soft GEI data to understand how the different ecosystem elements could work together most effectively. For this reason, we have developed a GEI Policy Stakeholder Engagement approach, which is designed to extract the soft, experience-based data to give insights into how the entrepreneurial ecosystem really works and what specific policy actions should be made to address bottlenecks.

To extract these soft insights, it is important to engage entrepreneurial ecosystem policy stakeholders who represent different elements of the ecosystem. Because these ecosystems are large and complex, it is likely that no single stakeholder has a full understanding of how they work. Therefore, it is important to allow each stakeholder to contribute their particular insights into what the ecosystem bottlenecks are and how they really work, perhaps by organizing stakeholder workshops. We have developed a stakeholder facilitation process designed to achieve exactly this purpose with the hard GEI data, which suggests that it is possible to organize a coherent, facilitated debate of the analysis to determine which of the bottlenecks are real and how they actually function.

For example, the GEI analysis suggested that Risk Capital was one bottleneck for the Scottish ecosystem. Discussions among the Scottish stakeholders confirmed that this was so, but they also noted an additional nuanced detail—that it was not the amount of funding that constrained Risk Capital but the fact that the capital tended to get stuck in portfolio companies because of limited exit opportunities. In other words, while they confirmed that Risk Capital was a bottleneck, they also learned that the real cause of this bottleneck was insufficient circulation of Risk Capital within the Scottish entrepreneurial ecosystem. This added considerable insight not easily achieved through the analysis of hard data alone, and also provided pointers for targeted policy action. By helping to extract such soft insights, the GEI Policy Stakeholder Engagement process facilitates an evidence-based, coherent understanding of how a given country's entrepreneurial ecosystem really works, what the system-level priorities are, and how the policy actions to alleviate the bottlenecks should be designed, prioritized, and coordinated. Thus, when combined with the GEI methodology, the GEI Policy Stakeholder Engagement process provides a useful platform for designing and operationalizing entrepreneurial ecosystem policies.

The GEI Policy Stakeholder Engagement Process comprises several steps:

1. Use the GEI analysis to identify possible bottlenecks in the country's entrepreneurial ecosystem.
2. Examine each bottleneck more closely in order to understand how it really works. To do this, it is important to engage with a group of policy stakeholders who can offer complementary insights into the inner workings of the entrepreneurial ecosystem. It is critical that the discussions be facilitated competently in order to draw out balanced insights and maintain coherence.
3. Conduct a causal analysis of how a bottleneck works by drawing on different sources of qualitative and quantitative data, thereby enabling a coherent discussion on how to alleviate the bottleneck.

4. Design and implement specific, coordinated policy actions to alleviate the country's ecosystem bottlenecks, and use the GEI to help set performance improvement targets.
5. Once consensus has been achieved about what the ecosystem's most pressing bottlenecks are and the associated policy priorities, an action stage should follow. This stage should focus on implementing specific, targeted policy actions collectively designed to bring about a real and tangible change in the ecosystem dynamic. This last stage can (and, in most cases, should) last for several years in order to ensure that it has a lasting impact.

Used this way, the GEI and the policy facilitation process can provide a powerful platform to identify and implement real, long-lasting change in how entrepreneurial ecosystems work. Our experiences in countries such as Scotland and Estonia suggest that the approach can identify both key pressure points on entrepreneurial ecosystems and ways to address them.

At present, most entrepreneurship policy initiatives are still implemented without much coordination or with coordination that is limited to different initiatives within the same domain (e.g., alternative policies to provide funding for small and medium-sized firms). Typically, the aim of such coordination is to avoid overlap in policy initiatives that address the same need, such as financing. While such coordination helps avoid the waste of resources that stems from a duplication of effort, it also fails to create and exploit synergies that might result from the kind of dynamic, mutually reinforcing interactions that bring entrepreneurial ecosystems to life. Today, coordinated entrepreneurship policy still primarily refers to avoiding overlap, rather than to maximizing the positive feedback and synergies between complementary actions. For entrepreneurship policies to nurture and facilitate entrepreneurial ecosystems effectively, policymakers must become more aware of how the different elements of these ecosystems interact. For example, the proliferation of government-sponsored venture capital programs has given rise to complaints in some countries that the real bottleneck is no longer scarce venture funding but the dearth of fundable management teams and innovative business concepts. If there are too few innovative, high-potential startups, venture capital initiatives will address the wrong bottlenecks. In an ecosystems approach to entrepreneurship policy, attention is paid to such bottlenecks and policy actions are coordinated to maximize positive synergies across complementary initiatives. This level of coordination is still missing in entrepreneurship policy today. The GEI platform, when appropriately implemented, should provide an effective tool for entrepreneurial ecosystem policymaking (Fig. 5.3).

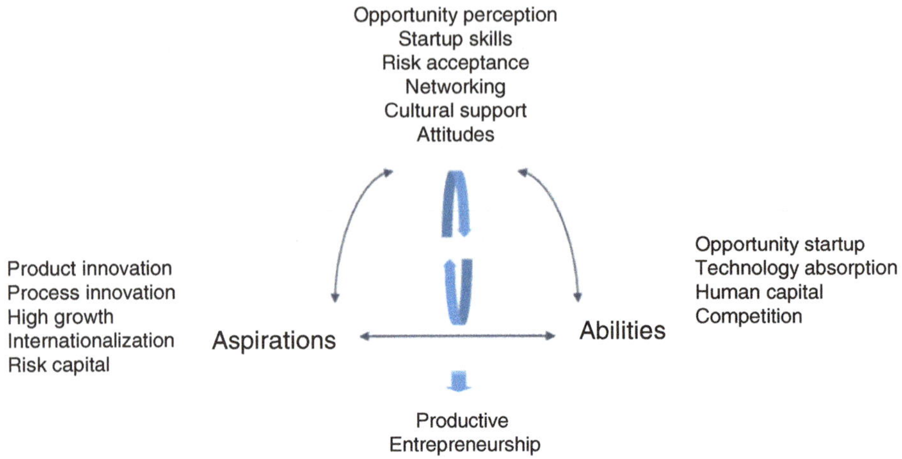

Fig. 5.3 Dynamic of national systems of entrepreneurship

Chapter 6
Methodology and Data Description

6.1 Introduction

In previous GEI publications, we have described the Global Entrepreneurship Index methodology in detail.[1] Here we describe the structure of the dataset, and a short summary of the GEI methodology.

6.2 The Structure of the Index

We have defined country-level entrepreneurship as "the dynamic, institutionally embedded interaction between entrepreneurial attitudes, entrepreneurial abilities, and entrepreneurial aspirations by individuals, which drives the allocation of resources through the creation and operation of new ventures." According to this definition, we propose four-level index building: (1) variables, (2) pillars, (3) sub-indices, and, finally, (4) the super-index. All three sub-indices contain several pillars, which can be interpreted as the quasi-independent building blocks of this entrepreneurship index. In this section, we describe the sub-indices and indicators. In the following section, we describe the variables. The three sub-indices of Attitudes, Abilities, and Aspirations constitute the entrepreneurship super-index, which we call the Global Entrepreneurship Index.

While the Abilities and Aspirations sub-indices (outlined below) capture actual entrepreneurship abilities and aspirations as they relate to nascent and startup business activities, the entrepreneurial attitudes (ATT) sub-index aims to identify the attitudes of a country's population as they relate to entrepreneurship. For example, the pillar known as Opportunity Perception Potential is essential to recognizing and exploring novel business opportunities. It is also critical to have the proper startup

[1] See Acs and Szerb (2009, 2012) and Acs, Szerb, and Autio (2013, 2014).

Z. Acs et al., *Global Entrepreneurship and Development Index 2016*,
SpringerBriefs in Economics, DOI 10.1007/978-3-319-63844-7_6

skills and personal networks to exploit these opportunities. Moreover, fear of failure to start a business can have a negative effect on entrepreneurial attitudes, even when opportunity recognition and startup skills exist. Entrepreneurial attitudes are believed to be influenced by the crucial institutional factors of market size, level of education, the level of risk in a country, the population's rate of Internet use, and culture, all of which are interaction variables of the indicator.

The entrepreneurial abilities (ABT) sub-index is principally concerned with measuring some important characteristics of the entrepreneur and the startup with high growth potential. This high growth potential is approached by quality measures, including opportunity motivation for startups that belong to a technology-intensive sector, the entrepreneur's level of education, and the level of competition. The country-level institutional variables include the freedom to do business, the technology adsorption capability, the extent of staff training, and the dominance of powerful business groups.

The entrepreneurial aspirations (ASP) sub-index refers to the distinctive, qualitative, strategy-related nature of entrepreneurial activity. Entrepreneurial businesses are different from regularly managed businesses, thus it is particularly important to be able to identify the most relevant institutional and other quality-related interaction variables. The newness of a product and of a technology, internationalization, high growth ambitions, and informal finance variables are included in this sub-index. The institutional variables measure the technology transfer and R&D potential, the sophistication of a business strategy, the level of globalization, and the depth of capital market.

By applying the Penalty for Bottleneck approach, the GEI methodology captures the notion that systems, by definition, comprise multiple components, and that these components co-produce system performance. These are defining characteristics of any system, which simple summative indices fail to capture. In a simple summative index, each system component contributes directly and independently to system performance. In the context of entrepreneurship, this would mean, for example, that a national measure of education would, directly and independent of other system components, contribute to "national entrepreneurship," while in reality we know that education cannot contribute much to a country's entrepreneurial performance if individuals fail to act. On the other hand, if education were absent, the economic potential of entrepreneurial entries would be severely constrained. Moreover, even if both education and agency were present, country-level entrepreneurial performance would be constrained if, for example, growth aspirations were missing or if there were no financial resources available to feed the growth of new ventures. A simple summative index would fail to recognize such interactions, thereby ignoring crucial aspects of system-level performance.

6.3 The Individual Variables and Dataset

As mentioned previously, an entrepreneurship index should incorporate both individual-level and institutional/environmental variables. All individual-level variables are from the GEM survey. The institutional variables are obtained from various sources.

Table 6.1 The description of the individual variables used in the GEI

Individual variable	Description
Opportunity recognition	The percentage of the 18–64 aged population recognizing good conditions to start business next 6 months in area he/she lives,
Skill perception	The percentage of the 18–64 aged population claiming to possess the required knowledge/skills to start business
Risk acceptance	The percentage of the 18–64 aged population stating that the fear of failure would not prevent starting a business
Know entrepreneurs	The percentage of the 18–64 aged population knowing someone who started a business in the past 2 years
Career	The percentage of the 18–64 aged population saying that people consider starting business as good career choice
Status	The percentage of the 18–64 aged population thinking that people attach high status to successful entrepreneurs
Career status	The status and respect of entrepreneurs calculated as the average of Career and Status
Opportunity motivation	Percentage of the TEA businesses initiated because of opportunity startup motive
Technology level	Percentage of the TEA businesses that are active in technology sectors (high or medium)
Educational level	Percentage of the TEA businesses owner/managers having participated over secondary education
Competitors	Percentage of the TEA businesses started in those markets where not many businesses offer the same product
New product	Percentage of the TEA businesses offering products that are new to at least some of the customers
New tech	Percentage of the TEA businesses using new technology that is less than 5 years old average (including 1 year)
Gazelle	Percentage of the TEA businesses having high job expectation average (over 10 more employees and 50% in 5 years)
Export	Percentage of the TEA businesses where at least some customers are outside country (over 1%)
Informal investment mean	The mean amount of 3-year informal investment
Business angel	The percentage of the population aged 18–64 who provided funds for new business in past 3 years, excluding stocks and funds, average
Informal investment	The amount of informal investment calculated as INFINVMEAN BUSANG

The full list and description of the applied GEM individual variables can be seen in Table 6.1.

For the 2016 GEI publication we used 2013–2014 or previous years' Global Entrepreneurship Monitor individual data. For the individual variable calculation, we include 499,136 individuals from 98 countries of the GEM Adult Population Survey; 69 countries' individual data are from the years 2013–2014, and 29 countries have individual data from the pre-2013 years. We estimated the individual variables for 34 countries by using nearby and similar countries' GEM Adult Population Survey data.

Since the availability of the institutional data also limited the selection of the countries, we could involve only those nations that participated in the World Economic Forum 2013–2014 or 2014–2015 Global Competitiveness Report (GCR) survey. Some GCR countries were left out because of the lack of similar or nearby GEM countries. The size of the sample in different years, the participating countries and the calculation of the individual variables, including the 37 non-GEM countries, are also reported in Table 6.2. All analyses of countries having data older than 2012 and based on estimation should be handled with caution.

6.4 The Institutional Variables and Dataset

Since the GEM lacks the necessary institutional variables, we complement individual variables with other widely used relevant data from Transparency International (Corruption Perception Index), UNESCO (tertiary education enrollment, GERD), World Economic Forum (domestic market size, business sophistication, technology absorption and technology transfer capability, staff training, market dominance), International Telecommunication Union (Internet usage), The Heritage Foundation and World Bank (economic freedom), the United Nations (urbanization index), the KOF Swiss Economic Institute (economic globalization), Coface (business climate risk), and Groh, Liechtenstein, and Lieser (2012; depth of capital market).

In this version, we apply the most recent institutional variables available on January 31, 2015. The full description of the institutional variables, their sources, and the year of the survey can be found in Table 6.3.

6.5 Missing Variables and Data Imputations

Since our basic individual data are provided by the GEM, participation in the GEM survey determines the potential list of countries and sample size. However, there is another potential limitation, the availability of institutional data. Because seven out of our fourteen institutional variables are from the GCI, it is particularly important to have these variables. While there were five additional countries in the GEM 2014 surveys, we had to cancel out Tonga, Vanuatu, the West Bank and Gaza Strip, Yemen, and Syria because of the lack of proper institutional variables.[2]

A few variables are missing for some countries. Since we did not want to drop any more countries from the sample, we estimated the missing data using expert techniques, as follows: the GERD measure lacked data for Angola, Bahrain, Bangladesh, Barbados, Belize, Benin, Cambodia, Cameron, Chad, Cote d'Ivoire, the Dominican Republic, Guyana, Lebanon, Libya, Mauritania, Namibia, Oman,

[2] Some may not consider the West Bank and Gaza Strip an independent country. Tonga and Vanuatu are tiny countries, and Yemen and Syria have been engaged in civil war over the last few years.

Table 6.2 The distribution of the sample by countries and the calculation of the individual variables

Country/year	2009	2010	2011	2012	2013	2014	Individual variable way of calculation
Albania							Average of Bosnia and Macedonia
Algeria				4984	2497		Average of 2012–2013
Angola					2049	2028	Average of 2013–2014
Argentina					1867	2095	Average of 2013–2014
Australia						1823	2014 data
Austria				4548		4554	Average of 2012–2014 data
Bahrain							Same as Qatar
Bangladesh			1932				2011 data
Barbados					2302	2000	Average of 2013–2014
Belgium					2001	2004	Average of 2013–2014
Benin							Average of, Burkina Faso and Cameroon
Belize						2000	2014 data
Bolivia						2590	2014 data
Bosnia and Herzegovina					2004	2015	Average of 2013–2014
Botswana					2204	2146	Average of 2013–2014
Brazil					10,000	10,000	Average of 2013–2014
Brunei Darussalam							Average of Malaysia and Singapore
Bulgaria							Average of Romania and Macedonia
Burkina Faso						2850	2014 data
Burundi							Average of Burkina Faso Uganda and Cameroon
Cambodia							Average of Vietnam and Thailand
Cameroon						2087	2014 data
Canada					2648	2037	Average of 2013–2014
Chad							Average of Burkina Faso Uganda and Cameroon

(continued)

Table 6.2 (continued)

Country/year	2009	2010	2011	2012	2013	2014	Individual variable way of calculation
Chile					5760	5375	Average of 2013–2014
China					3634	3647	Average of 2013–2014
Colombia					3400	3691	Average of 2013–2014
Costa Rica				2041		2057	Average of 2012–2014 data
Côte d'Ivoire							Average of Burkina Faso Uganda and Cameroon
Croatia					2000	2000	Average of 2013–2014
Cyprus							Same as Greece
Czech Republic					5009		2013
Denmark				2217		2008	Average of 2012–2014 data
Dominican Republic	2007						2009
Ecuador					1818	1834	Average of 2013–2014
Egypt				2501			2012
El Salvador				1905		2014	Average of 2012–2014 data
Estonia					1741	2036	Average of 2013–2014
Ethiopia				3003			2012
Finland					2005	2005	Average of 2013–2014
France					1567	1567	Average of 2013–2014
Gabon							Average of Namibia and Botswana
Gambia							Average of Burkina Faso Uganda and Cameroon
Georgia						1648	2014 data
Germany					5995	4311	Average of 2013–2014
Ghana				2213	2100		Average of 2012–2013
Greece					2000	2000	Average of 2013–2014
Guatemala					2138	2158	Average of 2013–2014

Table 6.2 (continued)

Country/year	2009	2010	2011	2012	2013	2014	Individual variable way of calculation
Guyana							Same as Suriname
Honduras							Average of Guatemala and Panama
Hong Kong	2000						2009
Hungary					2000	2003	Average of 2013–2014
Iceland		1684					2010 data
India					3000	3360	Average of 2013–2014
Indonesia					4500	5520	Average of 2013–2014
Iran					3633	3352	Average of 2013–2014
Ireland					2002	2000	Average of 2013–2014
Israel				2005	2039		Average of 2012–2013
Italy					2052	2000	Average of 2013–2014
Jamaica					2246	2637	Average of 2013–2014
Japan					2000	2006	Average of 2013–2014
Jordan	2006						2009
Kazakhstan						2099	2014 data
Kenya							Average of Burkina Faso Uganda and Cameroon
Korea				2000	2000		Average of 2012–2013
Kuwait							Same as Qatar
Lao PDR							Average of Vietnam and Thailand
Latvia				2000	2000		Average of 2012–2013
Lebanon	2000						2009
Liberia							Average of Burkina Faso Uganda and Cameroon
Libya					2246		2013
Lithuania					2000	2000	Average of 2013–2014
Luxembourg					2005	2074	Average of 2013–2014

(continued)

Table 6.2 (continued)

Country/year	2009	2010	2011	2012	2013	2014	Individual variable way of calculation
Macedonia				2003	2000		Average of 2012–2013
Madagascar							Average of Burkina Faso Uganda and Cameroon
Malawi				1847	2094		Average of 2012–2013
Malaysia					2000	1999	Average of 2013–2014
Mali							Average of Burkina Faso Uganda and Cameroon
Mauritania							Average of Burkina Faso Uganda and Cameroon
Mexico					2798	2587	Average of 2013–2014
Moldova							Average of Romania and Russia
Montenegro		2000					2010
Morocco	1500						2009
Mozambique							Average of Burkina Faso Uganda and Cameroon
Myanmar							Average of Vietnam and Thailand
Namibia				1959	1938		Average of 2012–2013
Netherlands					2441	1836	Average of 2013–2014
Nicaragua							Average of Guatemala and Panama
Nigeria				2651	2604		Average of 2012–2013
Norway					2000	2000	Average of 2012–2013
Oman							Same as Qatar
Pakistan			2002	2000			Average of 2011–2012
Panama					2004	2005	Average of 2013–2014
Paraguay							Average of Bolivia, Ecuador and Peru
Peru					2075	2078	Average of 2013–2014

Table 6.2 (continued)

Country/year	2009	2010	2011	2012	2013	2014	Individual variable way of calculation
Philippines					2499	2000	Average of 2013–2014
Poland					2000	2001	Average of 2013–2014
Portugal					2003	2005	Average of 2013–2014
Puerto Rico					1610	1995	Average of 2013–2014
Qatar						4269	2014 data
Romania					2021	1998	Average of 2013–2014
Russia					2029	2001	Average of 2013–2014
Rwanda							Average of Burkina Faso Uganda and Cameroon
Saudi Arabia		1957					2010 data
Senegal							Average of Burkina Faso Uganda and Cameroon
Serbia	1766						2009 data
Sierra Leone							Average of Burkina Faso Uganda and Cameroon
Singapore					1998	2004	Average of 2013–2014
Slovak Republic					2007	2000	Average of 2013–2014
Slovenia					2002	2004	Average of 2013–2014
South Africa					3133	3350	Average of 2013–2014
Spain					24,600	25,000	Average of 2013–2014
Sri Lanka							Average of India and Pakistan
Suriname					2074	2006	Average of 2013–2014
Swaziland							Average of Namibia and Angola
Sweden					1820	1889	Average of 2013–2014
Switzerland					1588	1895	Average of 2013–2014
Taiwan					2007	2000	Average of 2013–2014

(continued)

Table 6.2 (continued)

Country/year	2009	2010	2011	2012	2013	2014	Individual variable way of calculation
Tanzania							Average of Burkina Faso Uganda and Cameroon
Thailand					2362	2059	Average of 2013–2014
Trinidad and Tobago					1787	1769	Average of 2013–2014
Tunisia				2000			2012 data
Turkey				2401	32,945		Average of 2012–2013
Uganda					2513	2112	Average of 2013–2014
Ukraine							Average of Russia and Romania
United Arab Emirates			3029				2011 data
United Kingdom					9012	1572	Average of 2013–2014
United States					4266	2840	Average of 2013–2014
Uruguay					1620	1616	Average of 2013–2014
Venezuela			1888				2011 data
Vietnam					2000	2000	Average of 2013–2014

Qatar, Rwanda, Suriname, Swaziland, and Venezuela. In these cases, other government sources and data from similar nearby countries provided adequate estimates. KOF globalization index data for Libya, Hong Kong, Puerto Rico, and Taiwan are estimated similarly to the GERD, by applying nearby country data points. Puerto Rico's business freedom dataset is the same as the US. All the other data are available for all countries; therefore, we believe that these rough estimates do not influence our results noticeably.[3]

6.6 Calculating the Scores

The GEI scores for all the countries are calculated according to the following eight points.

[3] In order to check potential bias, the index was calculated without these countries; however, the GEI values and the rank order of the involved countries were basically unchanged.

Table 6.3 The description and source of the institutional variables used in the GEI

Institutional variable	Description	Source of data	Data availability
Domestic market	Domestic market size that is the sum of gross domestic product plus value of imports of goods and services, minus value of exports of goods and services, normalized on a 1–7 (best) scale data are from the World Economic Forum Competitiveness	World Economic Forum	The Global Competitiveness Report 2014–2015, p. 514
Urbanization	Urbanization that is the percentage of the population living in urban areas, data are from the Population Division of the United Nations, 2014 revision	United Nations	http://esa.un.org/unpd/wup/DataSources/
Market agglomeration	The size of the market: a combined measure of the domestic market size and the urbanization that later measures the potential agglomeration effect. Calculated as domestic market [a] urbanization	Own calculation	–
Tertiary education	Gross enrollment ratio in tertiary education, 2013 or latest available data.	UNESCO	http://data.uis.unesco.org/?queryid=142
Business risk	The business climate rate "assesses the overall business environment quality in a country…It reflects whether corporate financial information is available and reliable, whether the legal system provides fair and efficient creditor protection, and whether a country's institutional framework is favorable to intercompany transactions" (http://www.trading-safely.com/). It is a part of the country risk rate. The alphabetical rating is turned to a seven-point Likert scale from 1 (D rating) to 7 (A1 rating). December 31, 2014 data	Coface	http://www.coface.com/Economic-Studies-and-Country-Risks/Comparative-table-of-country-assessments
Internet usage	The number of Internet users in a particular country per 100 inhabitants, 2014 data	International Telecommuni-cation Union	http://www.itu.int/en/ITU-D/Statistics/Pages/stat/default.aspx
Corruption	The Corruption Perceptions Index (CPI) measures the perceived level of public-sector corruption in a country. "The CPI is a 'survey of surveys', based on 13 different expert and business surveys." (http://www.transparency.org/policy_research/surveys_indices/cpi/2009) overall performance is measured on a ten-point Likert scale. Data are from 2014.	Transparency International	http://www.transparency.org/cpi2014

(continued)

Table 6.3 (continued)

Institutional variable	Description	Source of data	Data availability
Economic freedom	"Business freedom is a quantitative measure of the ability to start, operate, and close a business that represents the overall burden of regulation, as well as the efficiency of government in the regulatory process. The business freedom score for each country is a number between 0 and 100, with 100 equaling the freest business environment. The score is based on 10 factors, all weighted equally, using data from the World Bank's *Doing Business* study." (http://www.heritage.org/Index/pdf/Index09_Methodology.pdf). Data are from 2013.	Heritage Foundation/ World Bank	http://www.heritage.org/index/explore
Tech absorption	Firm-level technology absorption capability: "Companies in your country are (1 = not able to absorb new technology, 7 = aggressive in absorbing new technology)"	World Economic Forum	The Global Competitiveness Report 2014–2015, p. 507
Staff training	The extent of staff training: "To what extent do companies in your country invest in training and employee development? (1 = hardly at all; 7 = to a great extent)"	World Economic Forum	The Global Competitiveness Report 2014–2015, p. 463
Market dominance	Extent of market dominance: "Corporate activity in your country is (1 = dominated by a few business groups, 7 = spread among many firms)"	World Economic Forum	The Global Competitiveness Report 2014–2015, p. 467
Technology transfer	These are the innovation index points from GCI: a complex measure of innovation, including investment in research and development (R&D) by the private sector, the presence of high-quality scientific research institutions, the collaboration in research between universities and industry, and the protection of intellectual property	World Economic Forum	The Global Competitiveness Report 2014–2015, p. 20
GERD	Gross domestic expenditure on R&D (GERD) as a percentage of GDP, year 2013 or latest available data; Puerto Rico, Dominican Republic, United Arab Emirates, and some African countries are estimated using regional or nearby country data.	UNESCO	http://stats.uis.unesco.org/unesco/TableViewer/tableView.aspx?ReportId=2656

Institutional variable	Description	Source of data	Data availability
Business strategy	Refers to the ability of companies to pursue distinctive strategies, which involves differentiated positioning and innovative means of production and service delivery	World Economic Forum	The Global Competitiveness Report 2014–2015, p. 20
Globalization	A part of the Globalization Index measuring the economic dimension of globalization. The variable involves the actual flows of trade, foreign direct investment, portfolio investment, and income payments to foreign nationals, as well as restrictions of hidden import barriers, mean tariff rate, taxes on international trade, and capital account restrictions. Data are from the 2013 report and based on the 2011 survey. http://globalization.kof.ethz.ch/	KOF Swiss Economic Institute	Dreher, Axel (2006): "Does Globalization Affect Growth? Evidence from a new Index of Globalization," *Applied Economics 38*, 10: 1091–1110.
Depth of Capital Market	The depth of capital market is one of the six sub-indices of the Venture Capital and Private Equity Index. This variable is a complex measure of the size and liquidity of the stock market, level of IPO, M&A, and debt and credit market activity. Note that there were some methodological changes over the 2006–2014 time period, so comparison to previous years is not perfect. The dataset is provided by Alexander Groh.[a] For missing data nearby country data used. For countries having estimated individual data, DCM data are the same way as it is in the case of individual variables (see Table 6.2 last column)	EMLYON Business School, France and IESE Business School, Barcelona, Spain	Groh et al. (2012)

[a]Special thanks to Alexander Groh and his team for providing the Depth of Capital Market data

1. ***The selection of variables:*** We start with the variables that come directly from the original sources for each country involved in the analysis. The variables can be at the individual level (personal or business) that are coming from the GEM Adult Population Survey, or the institutional/environmental level that are coming from various other sources. Altogether we use 16 individual and 15 institutional variables.
2. ***The construction of the pillars:*** We calculate all pillars from the variables using the interaction variable method; that is, by multiplying the individual variable with the proper institutional variable.
3. ***Normalization:*** Pillar values were first normalized to a range from 0 to 1, according to Eq. (6.1):

$$x_{i,j} = \frac{z_{i,j}}{\max z_{i,j}} \tag{6.1}$$

   for all j = 1…k, the number of pillars
   where $x_{i,j}$ is the normalized score value for country i and pillar j
   $z_{i,j}$ is the original pillar value for country i and pillar j
   max $z_{i,j}$ is the maximum value for pillar j

4. ***Capping:*** All index building is based on a benchmarking principle. We selected the 95th percentile score adjustment, meaning that any observed values higher than the 95th percentile are lowered to the 95th percentile. For the 132 countries in our dataset, we use the benchmarks values from the full dataset, which contains all the 629 observations made over the 2002–2014 time period.
5. ***Average pillar adjustment:*** The different averages of the normalized values of the indicators imply that reaching the same indicator values requires different effort and resources. Since we want to apply the GEI for public policy purposes, the additional resources for the same marginal improvement of the indicator values should be the same for all indicators. Therefore, we need a transformation to equate the average values of the components. Eq. (6.2) shows the calculation of the average value of pillar *j*:

$$\bar{x}_j = \frac{\sum_{i=1}^{n} x_{i,j}}{n} \tag{6.2}$$

We want to transform the $x_{i,j}$ values such that the potential minimum value is 0 and the maximum value is 1:

$$y_{i,j} = x_{i,j}^{k} \tag{6.3}$$

where k is the "strength of adjustment", the k -th moment of X_j is exactly the needed average, $\bar{y}_j$. We have to find the root of the following equation for k

$$\sum_{i=1}^{n} x_{i,j}^{k} - n\overline{y}_j = 0 \tag{6.4}$$

It is easy to see, based on previous conditions and derivatives, that the function is decreasing and convex, which means it can be solved quickly using the well-known Newton-Raphson method with an initial guess of 0. After obtaining k, the computations are straightforward. Note that if

$$\begin{aligned} \overline{x}_j &< \overline{y}_j \quad k < 1 \\ \overline{x}_j &= \overline{y}_j \quad k = 1 \\ \overline{x}_j &> \overline{y}_j \quad k > 1 \end{aligned}$$

then k is thought of as the strength (and direction) of adjustment.

The adjusted pillar values are calculated for all the 2002–2014 time period; these values and this distribution are applied for the 132 countries in the GEI 2016 edition. It means that the average adjusted pillar values of the countries that participated in the 2014 GEM cycle are exactly same in the 2002–2014 dataset and in the 2016 GEI edition. Note that, of the individual variables of the 132 countries in the GEI 2016 edition, 69 are from the 2013 survey, 29 are from earlier GEM surveys, and 34 are estimates.

6. ***Penalizing:*** After these transformations, the PFB methodology was used to create indicator-adjusted PFB values. We define our penalty function as follows:

$$h_{(i),j} = \min y_{(i),j} + \mathrm{a}\left(1 - e^{-\mathrm{b}\left(y_{(i)j} - \min y_{(i),j}\right)}\right) \tag{6.5}$$

where $h_{i,j}$ is the modified, post-penalty value of pillar j in country i
$y_{i,j}$ is the normalized value of index component j in country i
y_{min} is the lowest value of $y_{i,j}$ for country i.
i = 1, 2,……n = the number of countries
j = 1, 2,…….m = the number of pillars
$0 \leq$ a, b ≤ 1 are the penalty parameters, the basic setup is a = b = 1

7. The pillars are the basic building blocks of the sub-index: Entrepreneurial Attitudes, Entrepreneurial Abilities, and Entrepreneurial Aspirations. The value of a sub-index for any country is the arithmetic average of its PFB-adjusted pillars for that sub-index, multiplied by 100. The maximum value of the sub-indices is 100, and the potential minimum is 0, both of which reflect the relative position of a country in a particular sub-index.

$$ATT_i = 100\sum_{j=1}^{5} h_j \quad (6.6a)$$

$$ABT_i = 100\sum_{j=6}^{9} h_j \quad (6.6b)$$

$$ASP_i = 100\sum_{j=10}^{14} h_j \quad (6.6c)$$

where $h_{i,j}$ is the modified, post-penalty value of pillar j in country i
i = 1, 2,……n = the number of countries
j = 1, 2,…….14 = the number of pillars

8. The super-index, the Global Entrepreneurship Index, is simply the average of the three sub-indices. Since 100 represents the theoretically available limit, the GEI points can also be interpreted as a measure of the efficiency of the entrepreneurship resources

$$GEI_i = \frac{1}{3}\left(ATT_i + ABT_i + ASP_i\right) \quad (6.7)$$

where i = 1, 2,……n = the number of countries.

Starting this year, we report not only the GEI scores but also the associated measurement error terms for those countries that have participated in the GEM survey (see Chap. 3). It is impossible to make an error calculation for the countries that have only estimated individual data. The report of the confidence intervals is important in two respects. First, when comparing different countries, we can see if the differences in the two countries' GEI scores are significant or not. Based on the 2016 GEI scores, the GEI scores of the first five countries—the United States, Canada, Australia, Denmark, and Sweden—do not differ significantly. However, the GEI score difference is significant between the US in first place and Taiwan in sixth. Second, from year to year we can see if changes in the GEI scores are significant, or if they perhaps are due to measurement error. For example, the United Kingdom was ranked 4th, with a GEI score of 72.7 in 2015. By 2016 the UK GEI score decreased to 67.7. The confidence interval of the GEI score was 68.2–77.2 in 2015, and 63.5–71.8 in 2016. Since they overlap, we cannot exclude the possibility that the drop of the UK GEI score is due to measurement error and not a real change.

The confidence interval calculation is based on the error terms of the Total Early-Phased Entrepreneurship Activity index, as reported by the GEM each year. An important note is that the real measurement error is unknown, since we use many data from different sources for which confidence intervals are not currently available. Keep in mind that the real measurement errors are higher than the values reported here.

6.7 The Underlying Structure of the Data (Reflecting the Full 2002–2014 Dataset)

While the number of composite indicators has been increasing over the last few decades, some index creators pay little attention to the interrelationship between the different variables. Although the PFB methodology provides a practical solution for how to take this interrelationship into account, it does not save us from examining the underlying structure of the data. It is particularly important to have a well-defined nested structure of the whole index. The arbitrary selection of the variables—in our case the pillars—would cause confusion, false interpretation, and, finally, a misleading policy interpretation. The OECD handbook of composite indicators recommends analyzing the dataset in two dimensions, pillars and countries.[4] We have already provided detailed analyses at the country level; here we are presenting a pillar-level analysis by calculating the common (Pearson) correlation coefficients. Since we have only estimated data from 34 countries, it is better to examine not the 132 countries involved in our analysis but the full 2002–2014 dataset, with 629 data points.

We report correlations between the normalized and average equated pillars, shown in Table 6.4, and the correlations between the normalized indicators after applying the PFB methodology, shown in Table 6.5. In general, significant and medium to high correlations exist between the pillars in both cases. Opportunity Perception has positive and insignificant correlation with some other pillars (Process Innovation). Moreover, the correlation between Internationalization and Opportunity Perception is negative and significant, but the correlation coefficient is only −0.09, which is weak.

The PFB pillars, as can be expected, improved the correlation, implying a closer relationship between the entrepreneurial features. The positive connection between the entrepreneurship pillars is vital for proper policy interpretation and suggestions. If the connection between the pillars were negative, it would have implied that one pillar can only be improved at the cost of the other pillar. In this case, the improvement of the weakest pillar value would not necessary to improve the GEI value. This is not the case.

There are other ways to check out the consistency of the dataset and the potentially strong connection between the pillars. Both the Kaiser-Meyer-Olkin measure of sampling adequacy and Bartlett's test of sphericity reinforce the fact that the 14 GEI pillars are closely correlated, and it is worth looking for a single complex measure.[5] The most popular test of the internal consistency of the pillars is based on the Cronbach Coefficient Alpha (c-alpha). The c-alpha value for the 14 pillars is 0.92 with the original data, and 0.95 after applying the PFB methodology; both are well

[4] OECD, 2008.

[5] The Kaiser-Meyer-Olkin measures for the original pillar values are 0.91 and 0.94 for the PFB-adjusted pillars, well above the critical value of 0.50. The Bartlett test is significant at the 0.000 level, excluding the possibility that the pillars are not interrelated.

Table 6.4 The correlation matrix between the normalized and average equated pillars (2002–2014 dataset)

		1	2	3	4	5	6	7	8	9	10	11	12	13	14
1	Opportunity Perception	1	.266**	.168**	.197**	.332**	.247**	.189**	.131**	.280**	.231**	0.04	.112**	-.093*	.177**
2	Startup Skills		1	.224**	.419**	.317**	.342**	.323**	.255**	.244**	.161**	.156**	.143**	.244**	.323**
3	Risk Acceptance			1	.515**	.721**	.711**	.609**	.619**	.532**	.488**	.660**	.418**	.525**	.608**
4	Networking				1	.630**	.599**	.469**	.484**	.488**	.419**	.463**	.266**	.444**	.560**
5	Cultural Support					1	.719**	.623**	.560**	.642**	.516**	.580**	.413**	.518**	.655**
6	Opportunity Startup						1	.593**	.657**	.592**	.460**	.568**	.361**	.508**	.589**
7	Technology Absorption							1	.597**	.480**	.482**	.704**	.529**	.512**	.605**
8	Human Capital								1	.486**	.543**	.591**	.517**	.466**	.628**
9	Competition									1	.491**	.455**	.234**	.424**	.512**
10	Product Innovation										1	.614**	.526**	.368**	.568**
11	Process Innovation											1	.501**	.536**	.647**
12	High Growth												1	.501**	.492**
13	Internationalization													1	.620**
14	Risk Capital														1

** Correlation is significant at the 0.01 level (2-tailed).

* Correlation is significant at the 0.05 level (2-tailed).
The number of observations= 425

Table 6.5 The correlation matrix between the indicators, sub-indices, and the GEI super-index after normalizing and applying the PFB method (2006–2012 dataset)

		2	3	4	5	6	7	8	9	10	11	12	13	14	15	16	17	18
1	Opportunity Perception	.431**	.396**	.396**	.526**	.677**	.447**	.404**	.365**	.483**	.483**	.428**	.297**	.310**	.159**	.400**	.375**	.536**
2	Startup Skills	1	.422**	.573**	.498**	.727**	.509**	.502**	.456**	.445**	.548**	.364**	.373**	.354**	.419**	.501**	.477**	.613**
3	Risk Acceptance		1	.646**	.803**	.834**	.790**	.706**	.715**	.664**	.824**	.617**	.746**	.547**	.643**	.712**	.774**	.857**
4	Networking			1	.729**	.842**	.705**	.610**	.621**	.620**	.730**	.568**	.602**	.444**	.581**	.673**	.680**	.792**
5	Cultural Support				1	.899**	.793**	.727**	.688**	.747**	.844**	.655**	.702**	.559**	.643**	.746**	.783**	.890**
6	ATTINDEX					1	.821**	.745**	.721**	.747**	.867**	.665**	.692**	.561**	.623**	.767**	.783**	.932**
7	Opportunity Startup						1	.699**	.756**	.707**	.904**	.604**	.682**	.500**	.630**	.699**	.739**	.870**
8	Technology Absorption							1	.696**	.617**	.868**	.605**	.772**	.637**	.627**	.711**	.793**	.852**
9	Human Capital								1	.625**	.888**	.657**	.687**	.627**	.604**	.732**	.781**	.847**
10	Competition									1	.831**	.622**	.601**	.420**	.566**	.640**	.676**	.796**
11	ABTINDEX										1	.712**	.788**	.631**	.695**	.798**	.858**	.964**
12	Product Innovation											1	.700**	.624**	.521**	.677**	.829**	.781**
13	Process Innovation												1	.605**	.644**	.742**	.874**	.835**
14	High Growth													1	.608**	.621**	.811**	.711**
15	Internationalization														1	.711**	.827**	.761**
16	Risk Capital															1	.890**	.869**
17	ASPINDEX																1	.936**
18	GEI																	1
	** Correlation is significant at the 0.01 level (2-tailed).																	
	The number of observations= 425																	

above the critical 0.7 threshold value.[6] In sum, all of these tests support the internal consistency of the structure as described with the 14 selected pillars.

6.8 Summary

In this chapter, we have described the index-building methodology and the dataset. The GEI, a complex index reflecting the multidimensional nature of entrepreneurship, consists of three sub-indices, 14 pillars, and 31 variables. While some researchers insist on simple entrepreneurship indicators, none of the previously applied measures was able to explain the role of entrepreneurship in economic development with a single indicator.

Our index-building logic differs from other widely applied indices in three respects: it incorporates both individual and institutional variables, it equates the 14 pillar values for equalizing the marginal effects, and it takes into account the weakest link in the system. The institutional variables can also be viewed as country-specific weighting factors. Moreover, institutional variables can balance out the potential inconsistency of the GEM data collection. The weakest link refers to the decreased performance effect of the bottleneck. Practically speaking, it means that the higher pillar values are adjusted to the weakest performing pillar value. While the exact measure of the penalty is unknown, meaning that the solution is not necessarily optimal, it still provides a better solution than calculating the simple arithmetic averages. Consequently, the newly developed PFB can be applied in cases where an imperfect substitutability exists among the variables and the efficiency of the system depends on the weakest performing variable. The method is particularly useful in making policy suggestions.

The GEM survey served as a source for the individual variables, which are calculated mainly from the 2013–2014 individual dataset, except for the 29 countries that only have data from previous years. Altogether, the sample includes 499,136 individuals from 98 countries. Individual data from 34 other countries are estimated by using similar or nearby country individual data, resulting in a sample size of 132 countries.

The availability of the institutional variables for all the countries has limited our selection possibilities. The proper interpretation of a particular institutional variable has been an important aspect of the selection. For example, the muddled interpretations of the effect of taxes on other entrepreneurship variables led to the exclusion of taxation. In all cases, we used the most recent institutional data available as of April, 30, 2014.

We summarized the index-building steps in eight points. Since these steps were described in full detail in the previous publications, we provided only a short description.[7]

[6] We have calculated the c-alpha values for each of the three sub-indices. Using the PFB-adjusted pillar values, the c-alpha scores are 0.86 (ATT pillars), 0.90 (ABT pillars), and 0.90 (ASP pillars).

[7] See Acs, Szerb, & Autio, 2014, ch. 6.

We have analyzed the underlying structure of the dataset in the variable level. The correlation coefficients, the Kaiser-Mayer-Olkin measures, and the Bartlett and c-alpha tests all suggested that the 14 pillars have a close relation to one another and that there is a place to construct a composite indicator. These tests were executed with the normalized original, as well as with the PFB adjusted variables. As expected, the PFB methodology improved the internal consistency of the dataset.

References

Acs, Z. J., & Szerb, L. (2009). The Global Entrepreneurship Index (GEINDEX). *Foundations and Trends in Entrepreneurship, 5*, 341–435.

Acs, Z. J., & Szerb, L. (2012). *Global Entrepreneurship Index* (p. 400). Cheltenham, UK: Edward Elgar.

Acs, Z. J., Szerb, L., & Autio, E. (2013). *Global Entrepreneurship Index* (p. 352). Cheltenham, UK: Edward Elgar.

Acs, Z. J., Szerb, L., & Autio, E. (2014, March 19). *The Global Entrepreneurship Index 2014*. Seattle: CreateSpace.

Groh, A., Liechtenstein, H., & Lieser, K. (2012). *The global venture capital and private equity country attractiveness index*. http://blog.iese.edu/vcpeindex/about/

Kolibri 360 GmbH
Ferdinand-Jühlke-Straße 7
99095 Erfurt, Deutschland
produktsicherheit@kolibri360.de